WHO'S GOT YOUR BACK?

Why We Need Accountability

By Matt Loehr and Cecil Murphey

ISBN 10 Digit: 1450532527
ISBN 13 Digit: 9781450532525
Library of Congress Control Number: 2010900945

Unless otherwise indicated, all Scripture quotations are taken from the *Holy Bible, New Living Translation*, copyright © 1996, 2004. Used by permission of Tyndale House Publishers, Inc., Wheaton, Illinois 60189. All rights reserved.

NIV—Scripture taken from the HOLY BIBLE, NEW INTERNATIONAL VERSION®. Copyright © 1973, 1978, 1984 by International Bible Society. Used by permission of Zondervan Publishing House. All rights reserved. The "NIV" and "New International Version" trademarks are registered in the United States Patent Trademark Office by International Bible Society. Use of either trademark requires the permission of International Bible Society.

NKJV—Scripture taken from the New King James Version. Copyright © 1979, 1980, 1982 by Thomas Nelson, Inc. Used by permission. All rights reserved.

Printed in the United States of America.

Designed by Nichole R. Wagner

Imagery used with permission from www.dreamstime.com.

MATT: For my original accountability partner, John Rios, and my bride, Pam.

CEC: For my wife and life companion, Shirley, and David Morgan, my accountability partner for 30 years.

CONTENTS

ACKNOWLEDGMENTS

To my co-author, Cec Murphey: Words cannot capture my gratitude toward you and your heart for all people. I am fortunate that God in his sovereignty allowed our paths to cross. You have made me a better author, a more responsible Christian, and a better man. I pray blessings on you for all you have done for me.

To Pam: Your support as my loving wife has been immeasurable. Thank you for the grace and mercy you have given me. Thank you for pushing me when I had nothing left. Thank you for modeling a godly wife for so many to follow.

To John Rios, my first accountability partner: I miss you and your weekly presence in my life. I cannot emphasize enough how you changed my life. It's doubtful that I would be in ministry today if it were not for you. I probably wouldn't even be walking with the Lord. The laughter, the tears, the probing and challenging, the love, and the brotherhood are all pieces to the puzzle of our friendship. Our experience birthed this book. Thank you for loving me like a brother. I pray blessings on you and your family.

To Scott Lehman, my informal accountability partner: God placed you in my life for a perfect time and a perfect season. Your encouragement is like no other. Thanks for holding my feet to the fire.

To Scott Schaefer, Rich Lively, and Steve Bray: I cherish my time with you. You helped me climb the ladder of life one more rung. It is because of you I kept moving up one notch.

To Craig and Janine Stichter: Your presence in my life was powerful even before I was walking with God. You care for people so much and always put others before yourselves. You are the only two friends who stuck with me when I walked away from my old life to a new life with God. Thank you for that. Thank you for loving me.

To my twin brother, Mike: You've been a built-in accountability partner since inside our mother's womb. Thanks for the 18 years of support you gave me when we worked together. Thanks for encouraging me so much when I launched into full-time ministry. Thanks for loving me unconditionally.

To my brother Nathan: You gave me countless hours of your time as a little boy. The trips to church, the tennis games, the hunting and fishing are all memories of accountability that at times went both ways. Thanks for being a big brother to me.

To my parents: For giving me volumes of lessons that have shaped me and guided me. Your unfailing love for each other paved the way for me to be a man of character. You are amazing people. I cannot think of anyone who has given so much and taken so little. You are the truest examples of godly, righteous, loving Christ-followers that I know. Thank you for raising me to fear and love God.

Chapter 1

WHY DO I NEED ACCOUNTABILITY?

I had grown up in a Christian home and I knew the difference between right and wrong. My parents taught me proper Christian behavior and biblical principles.

After I went to college, like many young people, I lost my way. College life sucked me into partying and careless living. I abandoned my faith. Deep in my heart I knew what I did was wrong, but I lacked the strength to resist the seductive life.

Every so often, I'd look in the mirror and commit to changing my ways. But no matter how hard I tried or how much I struggled, the change never lasted. *Why can't I stop? What's wrong with me?*

After college, my struggle continued until I found the cure for my emptiness: I found God again. This time, I made a serious commitment to live a pure life. I promised God I would cut out the clubbing and abstain from sex until I got married. I wanted God to be my only love. The relationship with my girlfriend had been built on physical attraction; I knew she would pull me away from God if I didn't make a clean break. To fulfill my promise to the Lord, I broke up with her.

I basked in my newfound feelings of mercy and peace. Life seemed clearer as I stood on my own moral feet. As I learned, however, giving my life to Jesus Christ didn't mean temptations disappeared or that I no longer struggled over doing the right thing.

My ex-girlfriend wanted us back together. Something about her voice—that soft, sultry voice—triggered sinful desires within me. For a few weeks, I summoned my willpower to resist. I wouldn't agree to meet no matter how often she called. I knew if I did, she'd lure me into the old life and away from God.

She continued to call regularly. With each phone call, my willpower slipped a little. Temptation overwhelmed me. *Who can help me?* I didn't know of anyone to whom I could talk.

About that time, my church began to promote accountability partners and I joined in the program—reluctantly. Through their campaign I learned an invaluable lesson about myself. In the past, I made commitments to God—and I was serious—but I hadn't been accountable to anyone for my actions. I had no one to watch my back.

To follow and fully obey God's will I needed someone who would hold me accountable for my actions. As the years passed, and I committed my life to several ministries, I learned that all of us need those who will stand with us. We need those people who care enough to guard our back.

A decision to follow Christ doesn't immunize us against the strategies Satan uses to distract us. *Without accountability—without a human to whom we must answer—it's easy to go astray and justify our actions.* We all have blind spots (another way to say we're sinners). We can excuse ourselves or find ways to justify our actions, but God knows. Jeremiah states the situation well with these words: "The human heart is the most deceitful of all things, and desperately wicked. Who really knows how bad it is? But I, the LORD, search all hearts and examine secret motives" (Jere.17:9–10a).

Even kids know how to rationalize their behavior to avoid taking blame. For example, stop a couple of boys on the playground who are fighting. Inevitably, one of them will say, "Well, if he hadn't…"

Adam excused his behavior in the garden by blaming Eve; she blamed the snake. That means we've inherited from our first ancestors the ability to defend our wrongdoing. That's why accountability is so important: When others commit themselves to listen to us objectively they're not emotionally entrenched in our problems. Therefore they can point out our poor reasoning and encourage us to make wiser choices.

Being answerable to God is a principle that starts with the first pages of the Bible. God gave Adam and Eve only one negative command: not to eat of one tree. They disobeyed and God forced them to face their disobedience, or we can say God made *them* responsible for their actions. Satan tempted, but they didn't have to listen and they didn't have to sin.

God put the principle of accountability into place right then. Accountability began in the Garden of Eden and will continue until the end of this world. None of us is exempt. The apostle Paul writes: "For we must all stand before Christ to be judged. We will each receive whatever we deserve for the good or evil we have done in this earthly body" (2 Cor. 5:10).

I want to make it clear that accountability or taking responsibility for our actions has been a divine principle all through biblical history. It's not a new church program or another fringe idea. Below are examples of God calling people to account from Eden until we reach heaven:

1. In the Old Testament, God repeatedly used prophets to rebuke kings and their people—and to admonish them to reclaim their life in God. I could summarize the message of all the prophets in one word: *Repent.* Those men (and a few women) functioned as the conscience of the nation. No matter how easily the people of God rationalized idol worship, stealing, lying, and sexual sins, the prophets cried out, "Repent!" They pleaded with the people to become accountable to God through obeying the Law of Moses.

2. Too often the people didn't listen. Jesus cried out, "O Jerusalem, Jerusalem, the city that kills the prophets and stones God's messengers!" (Matt. 23:37a). Jerusalem was the center of Jewish worship; the leaders of the faith lived there and taught there. But simply being inside a holy place didn't make a difference. In the Sermon on the Mount, Jesus said several times, "You have heard it said," and gave the oral teaching of the leaders of the Jewish faith. He went on to add, "But I say."

For example, five times in Matthew chapter 5, Jesus says, in effect, "You've been taught one way and assume you get by with following rules. If you truly want to live a holy life…" (See 5:21, 27, 31, 33, 38, 43.)

3. Jesus made people responsible for their actions. One time, Jesus told his disciples that he would suffer and be killed by Jewish leaders. Peter "took him aside and began to reprimand him for saying such things" (Matt. 16:22a).

Peter was wrong. Possibly it was because of his selfish desire to have Jesus with them all through life, or perhaps he went into denial mode. Jesus answered him with these words, "Get away from me, Satan! You are a dangerous trap to me. You are seeing things merely from a human point of view, not from God's" (verse 23).

4. Another time, Jesus told a story we call the parable of the talents. A landowner gave a different sum of money to three servants. The landowner later came back and held those servants answerable for the way they had handled the money. (See Matt. 25:14–30.)

5. In the same chapter, Jesus told of the end of the world when everyone will stand in judgment before him. He separates the righteous from the unrighteous, *according to their daily actions.* This is the moment when the Lord faces them and they know they're held responsible (another word for accountable) for the way they've lived. (See Matt. 25:31–46.)

I don't mention these biblical accounts to frighten or discourage anyone, but to point out that God cares about us. Our choices matter and they determine the quality of our relationship with our Savior and with other people. God not only wants the best for us, but his Word, the Bible, is there to help us avoid going astray. However, we can't do it alone: We all need help.

In Jeremiah chapter 29, the prophet spoke from God when he wrote to the people who had been taken as prisoners to Babylon. He said they would have to stay in Babylon for seventy years. "'But then I will come and do for you all the good things I have promised, and I will bring you home again. For I know the plans I have for you,' says the Lord. 'They are plans for good and not for disaster, to give you a future and a hope'" (Jere. 29:10–11).

I want to make one thing clear: Although I use the term, *being responsible* and it's part of being accountable, the words aren't synonyms. Being responsible can push you to examine yourself and that can be the end. That happens when you admit your mistakes and accept your successes. Being accountable means you answer to someone other than yourself. That's what I want to emphasize.

Many people resist being accountable and it's easy to understand why. They view it as negative and restrictive. Sometimes it is exactly that. Accountability is like someone holding a mirror up to my face. "Look at this. This is who you are and you need to make changes."

My experience, and that of many others I've trained, is that a healthy, spiritual program of accountability makes us better people and more faithful Christians. A healthy relationship with one or more accountability partners enriches us and nudges us to live a life that honors God.

This chapter began with a question: Why do I need accountability? One of my favorite reasons is that it becomes a reality check on our lives. If we know we're accountable, it makes us more sensitive to our motives and more careful of our actions.

HERE ARE OTHER QUESTIONS:

Question: Is it possible for you to be a solo Christian? That is, just you and God?

Answer: That's possible.

Question: Is it possible to be a strong, solo Christian?

Answer: Not likely.

Here's an interesting verse: "The Lord now chose seventy-two other disciples and sent them ahead in pairs to all the towns and places he planned to visit" (Luke 10:2). Pairs. That means two people together. I believe he did it that way so one could strengthen the other. Each disciple would have someone to lean on when the heavy winds of oppression blew against them.

Here's a final question: If you want to serve Jesus Christ and you know that being accountable to someone else will help you mature spiritually, would you hesitate to get someone to watch your back?

Chapter 2

WHAT DOES ACCOUNTABILITY LOOK LIKE?

I believe strongly in accountability—and that's obvious all the way through this book. Over the past decade I participated in several experiments and accountability projects, and finally set up my own program. I'm convinced that we become strong, faithful Christians when we meet regularly with at least one other Christian with the purpose to share our life journeys together.

That is, we learn to open up to each other and speak freely of our ups and downs—the emotional, spiritual, physical, relational, and financial parts of life. We develop a relationship of trust that enables us to listen carefully to our accountability partner. I wrote *listen carefully* because this doesn't mean someone dictates to you or tells you how to live. It does mean another person walks with you and grabs you so that you don't stumble or get tripped up by your blind spots. Paul urged his readers, "Share each other's burdens, and in this way obey the law of Christ" (Gal. 6:2).

Together partners learn each other's strengths and weaknesses. They identify threats to their well-being. With love, they confront when necessary and with compassion expose wrong thinking. Accountability partners build action plans to develop healthy lives so that both of them grow closer to God.

When done correctly, my program provides a safe and loving relationship so you can share your needs, trials, problems, joys, failures, and victories. It helps you build a relationship where you can look in the mirror and know you're being true to yourself. You do the same thing for your partner. It's one of those delightful win-win relationships.

FOR WHOM IS ACCOUNTABILITY BEST SUITED?

I'll answer by asking another question: Who would benefit by meeting with a close, caring friend to discuss painful and distressing issues and come up with action plans to move forward?

The answer: every serious Christian.

No one is immune to weakness. No one is beyond temptation that drives us off course. All of us need someone who'll lovingly guide us away from destructive choices. Those bad choices may not be what we call big sins or harmful practices, but they're still desires that pull us from God. As one person said, "It can mean the difference between choosing the expedient and the wise, between the good and the best."

HOW DO YOU DISCOVER AND FOLLOW GOD'S WILL?

What is your life like now without accountability? Do you feel alone? If you had a terrible, urgent problem at 2:30 in the morning, is there someone you could call? Someone who would care, listen, and pray with you? Someone that you *knew* wanted only the best for you?

I ask that because I know what intentional accountability has done for me. For a long time, I didn't have anyone, so I know the difference. For several years my life was aimless, even after I became a Christian. I lacked the focus to stay on course. I had no one who could talk to me objectively. I met many people who would give me unwanted advice or who acted as if they knew the solution to every problem. They meant well, but *that's not accountability.* In an accountable relationship the other person listens without telling me how to run my life. And I do the same for others.

But until I discovered how the relationship works and was willing to try it, like many others, I thought I could make it on my own.

I was wrong.

If you're still not sure, here are a couple of things for you to consider. What about those times when you weren't sure what to do? You faced a decision and all your options seemed equally good. Or worse, they seemed equally bad. You were too close to the situation to be objective and couldn't determine the best route.

For example, several years ago my wife, Pam, met with Anna, a young woman who needed to make a career choice. Anna was blessed with musical talents and her family pushed her to go into a Christian music ministry. But she wanted to pursue a career in journalism. After they became accountability partners, Anna said, "I feel tugged in different directions. I want God's will. I want to respect my parents, and I also want to follow a vocation that will give me the most joy."

Pam listened for a long time and asked a few probing questions. Once she was sure she understood Anna's dilemma, she asked, "Can you back up and analyze the situation? What does God want you to do with your life?"

"I don't know," she said. "I can't get my head around the answer. Both options seem right."

Pam didn't have the answer and her purpose wasn't to solve Anna's problem. Her purpose was to encourage Anna to push aside the pressures and to decide for herself what she truly believed God wanted her to do with her life.

"What lights up your heart like a fully decorated Christmas tree?" Pam asked.

"The opposite of what everyone wants me to do. It's journalism."

Pam smiled and so did Anna.

"I've finally been able to say out loud where I want to go in my career," Anna said. "I've been caught up in listening to many other voices and denied what my heart tried to tell me." She allowed other voices to intrude and to block out the single, authoritative voice of God.

It's not always that simple or easy to come up with the right solution. I hope you noticed that Pam didn't tell Anna what to do. It had to be Anna's decision. If Pam had injected her opinion, she would have added another confusing voice to Anna's dilemma. The purpose of accountability isn't to offer advice, but to clarify the situation and help the other person make wise, healthy, and spiritual choices.

Accountability partners commit themselves to do what Pam did. She determined to stay with her friend. She nudged, probed, and asked questions until Anna herself was able to resolve the situation and knew it was the right thing for her to do.

It's even more than helping your partners see the right path to take. You also continue to encourage as the other moves forward. You stay with them as they plan the steps they will take. In turn, they make themselves responsible to report back to you on their decisions and their actions. That's when accountability becomes truly effective: When you tell the other what you will do and follow through on your self-promises.

Although Anna's parents were godly people, their desire to see her soar in a music ministry prevented their being objective. They wanted something good for her and believed she had the talent to accomplish *their desires*.

Anna felt emotionally trapped by trying to please them as she sought to discover God's will. She knew what they wanted and she needed someone to help her respond to the Holy Spirit's guidance to go in a different direction. She had the influence of godly parents telling her one thing, but her heart wasn't in it.

I didn't go into detail, but part of Anna's problem was that she kept asking herself, what's wrong with me? If music is the right thing for me, why do I hold back? Where's the joy in doing God's will?

Is it any wonder that she was confused? Until she spoke with Pam, Anna didn't have anyone with whom she could discuss the situation objectively. Anna's accountability partner did the one thing for her that no one else could: She listened without giving her answers. That's a powerful aid for any Christian who seeks to be faithful to God.

Most of us, like Anna, have a small circle of people who are close enough to influence us. Some of them may have God in their life. When they don't and we lean on them, it's often the blind leading the blind. They can't see through the darkness any better than we can. Or they may be believers but they're too close to the situation. Or they have opinions about the right thing to do and they may be wrong. It's extremely difficult for close friends to become accountability partners because they can rarely pull back from the friendship and look at situations objectively.

As part of a Christian community in America, we face many distractions—long work hours, childrearing responsibilities, television, church events, iPods, shopping, children's extracurricular activities, and the list seems to have no end. We live in a country with abundance and almost limitless options, but we lack *spiritual abundance*. It's difficult enough to find time to hear God's voice. If we don't set aside time to hear God speak, how can we discern what direction we should follow? It helps when we have someone we have learned to trust and who will stand beside us, nudge us, or push us through the noises, and help us hear the whisper of the Holy Spirit.

THINK ABOUT THESE THINGS

Here are a few questions for you to ponder. You don't have to write your answers, but I encourage you to think about them carefully. The first one is the most difficult to answer because you probably don't know the answer: *What is your purpose in life?* That is, why are you here on earth? It's not that you have to be able to explain to yourself or to anyone else, but prayerfully consider this. If God does everything with a purpose and each of us is alive and stays alive by what some call "divine providence," why are you here? If you had to make a statement to answer your purpose on earth, what would you say?

HERE ARE OTHERS:

* **What are your goals?**

* **What are your special abilities or talents? (We all have them.)**

* **Why did God give you those gifts? That is, what does the Holy Spirit want you to do with those abilities?**

We admire focused individuals who don't doubt their direction, those who never seem to veer off their chosen road. They have a peace about them, a confidence that they're walking on an ordained path. Isn't that the peace and confidence we want? And it is possible for you to have that deep sense of assurance.

Jesus said, "My purpose is to give them [us] a rich and satisfying life" (John 10:10b). Although that's Jesus' purpose for all of us, most of us have trouble hearing his voice. We have too many distractions around us and need those who can pull us aside as Pam did Anna.

In the book of Galatians, Paul discusses the fruit of the Spirit—the personal results of seeking the Holy Spirit's guidance. The fruit is "love, joy, peace, patience, kindness, goodness, faithfulness, gentleness, and self-control" (Gal. 5:22-23). Where is your love, joy, and peace? Where are the other fruit Paul mentions? They're not just a list of desirable traits; they're a list of spiritual qualities available to you and to me.

One reason I don't see the fruit of the Spirit is that too many Christians lack purpose. Many also dislike their church, fail in their marriage, detest their job, or succumb to secret temptations. We can usually trace those problems back to one source: They have no sense of divine direction or purpose. Without knowing what they're supposed to do on this earth, how can they fulfill God's divine purposes for them? How can they develop the fruit of the Spirit if they don't know why they're needed?

I've counseled hundreds of people, and I'm dismayed at how many numbly proceed through the humdrum assembly line of life. They go to work, attend church, and raise their family. But peace evades them; their soul aches; they silently yearn for more but don't even know how to define more or how to discover how to walk closer to God.

It saddens me when people can't tell me what they hope to be doing in five years. They have a GPS system that guides their cars down the correct road but don't seem to have anything that points them down the specific road God wants them to travel. They can go to MapQuest to get to a destination, but they don't seem able to navigate around spiritual roadblocks.

Accountability zeros in on our reason for being here on this earth. *Right now.* Accountability partners try to help the other discern God's will. With knowledge of that will, they plan actions and hold each other to those plans.

Here's my story of planning and being responsible to others. Through years of prayer and meeting with my accountability partner, I discerned that someday I would go into full-time ministry. When that day finally arrived, Pam and I took a leap of faith and left our lucrative jobs. Our future offered no promises of income and that might have deterred me. But one thing enabled me to step out: I knew my purpose; I had a plan to follow.

Almost immediately after I quit my job, a church asked me if I would pastor one of their campuses. I knew my answer. I said no.

"But what will you do for a job?" the church's executive pastor asked.

"I don't know," I said. "But I *do know* I'm supposed to dedicate myself to helping marriages succeed." I told him politely that pastoring wasn't my purpose.

Although foregoing steady income felt like jumping off a cliff into a dense fog with no idea what lay at the bottom, peace filled my soul when I said no. I knew what God wanted me to do.

Although it's not important to explain all the things that came together, I want to point out that God provided for our financial needs. My accountability partner guarded my back during that time. He would have spoken up if he had discerned that I was making wrong choices.

STRENGTH IN NUMBERS

According to something I heard on PBS[1], more than fifteen million Americans suffer from major depression, with 80 percent of them not currently receiving treatment. Furthermore, 90 percent of people who committed suicide had some type of diagnosable depressive disorder. People with major depression largely try to handle it the hard way—they try to go it alone.

When I heard those words, I wondered how many would be happier with accountability in their life. How many of those lives could have been saved if they had had a loving accountability partner?

You may not suffer from clinical depression but life is still difficult. At times you're probably confused and unsure which direction to follow. How could it be otherwise? That's how life works.

Are you one of those who say, "I wish I could disconnect from life for a little while. I just want a break from the pressure."? Or perhaps you don't like the way you live with constant anxiety and uncertainty filling your soul.

Here's the good news: You don't have to struggle with that by yourself. Regardless of whether depression is an issue or not, holding your pain inside isn't healthy. Those issues become more bearable when someone guards your back.

I can't give you a magic formula to abolish your struggles. But I can tell you that any burden is lighter if two or more people carry it. Imagine trying to carry a large, two-hundred-pound box—a box so large you can't get your arms around it. Would you rather carry that thing by yourself or enlist the help of one or two others who could distribute the load? The answer is obvious.

Here's an example of what I mean by sharing the load. Several years ago, three couples at our church, including Pam and me, considered leaving their jobs about the same time to go into full-time ministry. When we learned about each other, the six of us met occasionally and served as accountability partners to each other.

One couple, the Lehmans, tried to discern if God wanted them to leave Iowa and move to Tennessee. Leslie faced a lot of understandable fear about the loss of income. If she had to make that choice by herself, the fear might have become an overwhelming burden. Pam and Leslie spoke often and shared their fears. They bounced ideas off each other. They prayed, encouraged, and shed tears together. Leslie and Pam reminded each other that God had led them in specific directions. They encouraged each other in ways neither could have done alone.

For Leslie and Pam, the act of speaking openly about their fears, along with the encouragement and accountability they received, conquered the emotions that could have distracted them from God's will.

I mention this because it illustrates my point. When we reveal our burdens—whether painful struggles, difficult decisions, or tempting sins—we fight back against the things that spiritually distract. When we share the truth about ourselves, the burden becomes lighter.

Satan is a master of train derailments. He possesses means of obstruction that fit with your areas of weakness: fear, anger, love of money, ego, hopelessness, complacency, and pleasure seeking. Sometimes his distractions come looking like innocent events— even noble pursuits. Some thought I was wrong to turn down an opportunity to pastor. "That's doing God's work, isn't it?" someone said.

It was God's work, but it wasn't Matt's work.

The diversions might come in the form of a job promotion or relocation, or maybe through the needs of a friend or family member. Satan uses people, things, and ideas to lure us away from God. He whispers in our ear that certain things are okay, even desirable. But a trusted friend can often see through those unhealthy distractions and rationalizations. An accountability partner can say, "That doesn't sound right."

It seems odd that, as Christians, we would choose to go the lone-ranger route. But remember this when you think of going it alone: Even the Lone Ranger had Tonto. Batman had Robin. Gulliver had Friday. They were more powerful as a team.

God's most frequent tool in helping you and me is to use other people. In the Bible, his miracles and messages were delivered by chosen individuals—Moses parted the Red Sea. At the Jordan, nothing happened until the toes of the priests touched the water. Prophets delivered God's words of rebuke and the call for repentance.

And what about Jesus? He had a circle of Peter, James, and John and they were part of a select group of twelve. He had an even larger circle of disciples. One time the Bible says he sent out seventy disciples (Luke 10:1, 17). A number of women also followed him, and a small group of them stood at the cross when he died. If Jesus needed others, what makes you think you could make it on your own?

Here's another point that the New Testament mentions: There is strength in numbers. In Matthew 18:20, Jesus says, "For where two or three gather together as my followers, I am there among them." Of course he's always with us, but it's a way to affirm the strengthening presence of others. With Jesus among you and your partners, you gain strength and you receive insight on how to move forward.

Chapter 3

MUST I REVEAL MY SECRETS?

"Are you afraid of accountability?" Fifteen years ago, John Rios asked me that question.

"Me? Of course I'm not afraid."

He studied my face for several seconds before he added, "Then why aren't you interested in accountability?"

"Oh, it sounds fine, but it's not for me." I also didn't think it was important and told him, "It sounds like a phase the church is going through."

Months earlier, my church had started promoting the concept of accountability relationships and the members talked about it. Many got involved. *Accountability* became the buzzword, and I thought it was a religious fad. "Within a year no one will talk about it," I told someone.

I was wrong. The buzz didn't fade. The campaign grew into a vibrant, sustainable culture within our church. More than a year later, I still silently defended my decision. Why would I tell anyone else my secrets? Why should I have to tell someone else about my failures and mistakes? I convinced myself that God and I could handle everything, so I avoided learning the finer details about the program. Whenever somebody brought it up, my reaction was always the same: "It may be a good idea, but it's not for me."

It wasn't until John asked me point-blank about my fear.

Who me? I'm not afraid!

I reminded myself that I was a man with a new life in Christ. So why should I be afraid of anything? I even had support from the Bible: "Perfect love expels all fear. If we are afraid, it is fear of punishment, and this shows that we have not fully experienced perfect love" (1 John 4:18).

It's true that I struggled in several areas of my life, but God and I had everything under control. I confessed my sins to him; why should anybody else know the yucky stuff in my life? *I'm good with God. I'm walking the straight and narrow.*

But the more I thought about my many interior battles, the more I realized the truth. I was afraid, really afraid. John was right. *I wasn't afraid of punishment. I was afraid that others would know how imperfect I was. Exposing my secrets scared me.* I didn't want anyone to know about the bad stuff in my life.

I had experienced several months of what I call new-believer momentum. I had fallen in love with God again. I made many promises. The escape from my old life thrilled me. I didn't want to disturb that vibe by inviting someone else into my mess—letting him see the many little ways I went wrong or (worse) still failed regularly.

MONSTERS IN THE CLOSET

When I recognized my fear of letting someone inside my private world, I discovered it was the small sins—the extremely small ones—that troubled me the most. *Who wants someone to look into his heart and see all his shortcomings?*

My life hid many secrets like monsters in a closet. I wanted to keep that closet sealed shut. I didn't know what would happen if I cracked open the door and let the light inside. I didn't realize that by *letting in* the light I was *pushing out* the monster secrets.

Secrets don't have to be big to frighten us. We all battle *small* sins— jealousy, greed, anger, deception, small lies—things we strive to bury deep inside. Think of it this way. You know about those secrets; Jesus knows them. If you're like I was, you'll say to yourself, I can do just fine by keeping those secrets between Jesus and me.

As a new Christian, I tried to break my bad habits. I wanted to shed my non-Christian past as fast as possible. *What will people think of me if I come clean and they can see me as I am?* I didn't want to face the answer to that question. Instead, I wanted to hide parts of me so others would accept me as a mature, faithful, and extremely blessed Christian.

For instance, I struggled with arrogance. Deep down, I thought I was better than many others in our church. Especially in my corporate life, I was often insensitive to employees—at best, my attitude caused tension; at worst, my attitude pushed people to quit.

My callousness didn't limit itself to work, though, and I had damaged many relationships. I hated that part of my life. My Christian conversion offered a convenient way to run away from those things. Surely, God would set me free from every one of them immediately and forever.

As you may have guessed, it didn't work that way. Even as a Christian, I struggled with arrogance. I'd heard Christian leaders teach that if we leave a small sin unattended, it grows into something larger and even more damaging. Now I knew what they meant. I wanted people to respect me, especially my new church friends. If I disclosed the ugly truth, what would happen to that respect I wanted?

I didn't grasp that if we keep part of ourselves cloaked in darkness, it separates us from Jesus. He said, "...God's light came into the world, but people loved the darkness more than the light, for their actions were evil. All who do evil hate the light and refuse to go near it for fear their sins will be exposed" (John 3:19–20).

I still wasn't ready to let go. How could I come into the light if part of me longed for the darkness?

SECRETS DESTROY LIVES

As I pondered the idea of darkness, I thought of my childhood. When I was a kid, monsters in our closet often terrified me. I lay in bed, pulled the covers to my chin, and looked warily at the closet door. Fear snaked through my heart.

But what happened when my mother came in, opened the door, and turned on the light? That's when I discovered the objects in my closet weren't frightening. Once I understood that, I was at peace and able to fall asleep.

Maybe you feared the monsters of darkness when you went into the unlit basement or walked down a road with no street lights. In some form, most of us experience the fear of darkness. Yet when we faced those hidden monsters, they no longer held power over us. We can say the same about sins and secrets. It's not so much the sins, but it's the *secrets* that destroy lives.

Secrecy binds you and controls you. Once you expose your secrets to another human being, the chains break and you're free.

Another thing: Secrets don't stay hidden. They can't be stashed away—harmless and ignored. As Jesus said, "…Any kingdom divided by civil war is doomed. A town or family splintered by feuding will fall apart" (Matt. 12:25b). I'll say it this way: A soul divided between a hidden life and a public life can't survive. Secrets have ways of coming out—either directly or indirectly. You can choose between exposing them on your terms or you can let them be revealed on their terms.

When your secret sins are exposed publicly, they can cause catastrophic damage. Ask Jim Bakker, whose secret sins led him to prison. Ask Ted Haggard, who lost his job and reputation. Ask Achan who thought no one saw him steal gold from the destroyed city of Jericho.

Think about the story of David's great sins. As recorded in 2 Samuel 11, David gazed at and lusted for Bathsheba. David must have felt an inner warning within his heart, but his desire was so strong he was able to ignore the inner voice of conscience. If he'd talked to someone, an accountability partner, he could have exposed his secret lust and killed its growth.

Instead, he pursued a trail of destruction. His first sin led to the next when he slept with Bathsheba. That led to deception when he tried to get Bathsheba's husband, Uriah, to sleep with his wife to account for her pregnancy. Finally, he arranged Uriah's murder.

As with David, the first sin can appear small and insignificant. "I'm only looking at a beautiful woman," he might have said. People who have affairs tell lies, steal time or withhold energy from their employers, and lack commitment to their families. They have many opportunities to avoid that destructive path, but they choose to ignore the avenues of escape before they commit the sin.

Maybe not adultery or murder, but we've all done things that, deep down, we knew were wrong. We couldn't seem to help ourselves or we found ways to justify our actions. Later, shame or guilt prevented us from telling anyone.

All too often, the sin grows into something larger that eventually gets exposed. When Nathan confronted David, he told the king that God would punish him. Unlike David's sins done in secret, God would reveal the punishment in public. "You did it secretly, but I will make this happen to you openly in the sight of all Israel" (2 Sam. 12:12).

You may think you're finished with your secrets. "They're part of the past," you say. "And burying the past is the best thing to do." Sounds good that you're finished with the past, but as long as they stay hidden, your secrets are never finished with you. They find their way out into your consciousness. They plague you with fears and doubts. And, like David's secrets, they may be exposed to public view. Jesus said, "All that is secret will eventually be brought into the open, and everything that is concealed will be brought to light and made known to all" (Luke 8:17).

The casualties of secret sins aren't limited to the sinner. The web of wrong behavior entangles others. For David, God took the life of his son whom Bathsheba bore. For people like Jim Bakker and Ted Haggard, the damage extended to their families, their careers, and they caused stumbling for thousands who believed in them.

Even the rare individual who takes secrets to the grave hides those things at a price that includes lifetime struggles with shame, guilt, anger, and depression. Lifelong struggles damage relationships and careers. Perhaps worst of all, God stops using that person because of the deception. God cuts off the planned blessings.

That which you conceal is what enslaves you; what you reveal enables you to overcome.

Because I know the value and the blessings of having someone to watch my back, I can't talk about it enough. Sharing your secrets is healthy *when it's done in a safe, managed way*. Notice those last words: a safe, managed way. That's the heart of accountability, as I'll explain in later chapters.

With another Christian helping, praying, and offering objective insight, truth leads to healing. Concealing a secret means no one watches your back. No one supports you in your struggles. No one can offer an objective viewpoint.

ISN'T COMMITMENT TO JESUS CHRIST ENOUGH?

"If I've committed my life to Jesus and he's my best friend," someone asked me, "can't I confess my sins to him and be done with it? Shouldn't that be enough?"

Privately confessing your sins is important. Accountability partners don't suggest you stop. There are certainly things we want to bring only to God. But what if it's not enough? You need help if you confess to God and

- **you're still troubled,**

- **the guilt doesn't go away, or**

- **you continue doing the same things repeatedly.**

Having an accountability partner isn't the only way to win over such problems, but it works and also fulfills the biblical command, "Confess your sins to each other and pray for each other so that you may be healed. The earnest prayer of a righteous person has great power and produces wonderful results" (James 5:16).

Think of it this way: If something in your life is an ongoing problem, something that continues to trouble you, it means you haven't become victorious in that area. It means you need help. It means that even if it's a small thing, it's big enough to defeat you if you don't have someone to watch your back.

Another thing: It's easier to tune out God when it's just you and him. It's harder when it's you, God, and someone else. You can ignore that quiet voice that whispers a warning; you can't easily ignore a loving friend who speaks loudly and clearly.

Instead of thinking of someone guarding your back as a negative—which I did in the beginning—why not see the positive side? Because God loves you, he provides other people to stand with you. You don't have to fight the battle alone. Not only do you have the Lord, but you have another human being who expresses compassion and strength.

I once heard Charles Swindoll on the radio discuss the importance of other people in our spiritual lives. He said something like this: "You can tell how close people are to God by how close they are to others. God is in the business of people."

If you're into God, you're going to be into people—by serving them, but also by being served *by them*. If you're into God, you won't try to handle everything alone.

CONQUERING FEAR, SHARING SECRETS

In Ephesians 4, Paul tells believers to stop lying, to get rid of anger, quit stealing, and to cut the swearing and abusive language. The chapter ends with these words: "Get rid of all bitterness, rage, anger, harsh words, and slander, as well as all types of evil behavior. Instead, be kind to each other, tenderhearted, forgiving one another, just as God through Christ has forgiven you" (verses 31–32).

Most of us (probably all of us) have trouble with those things Paul mentioned. He not only tells us to excise them, but he goes on to talk about being in relationship with each other. Particularly notice his words, "...forgiving one another, just as God through Christ has forgiven you."

Here's how I see this. You sin and realize what you've done, so you repent and confess to God. It's over. *Or is it?*

What about next time? And the time after that? Can you handle it alone? *Have you handled it alone?*

My co-writer, Cec Murphey, says it this way. "I confess to another Christian. When that person says, 'I understand' or 'God forgives you,' it's like hearing God himself speak to me. It's God touching me through human hands."

Accountability provides a healthy, confidential place not only to confess, but also the opportunity to *know* we're forgiven.

As I've already mentioned, when my church first promoted accountability, I shunned it. But when I struggled to resist my ex-girlfriend and realized I was losing the battle, I decided to face my fear and give accountability a try.

"All right, John," I said. "I'm willing to try."

That's all it took: my willingness. John and I became accountability partners. We met regularly, and in the process we became good friends.

He frequently asked, "What are you dealing with right now?"

The first time I wasn't sure how much I could trust him. (We have to build trust.) I told him a few minor things.

John understood and helped me think through future actions. I tried to do the same for him. Each time we met, I trusted him a little more with my deep-seated struggles. To his credit, John pushed me with things beyond my failures—and I learned to do the same with him.

"What are your goals?" John once asked. "What kind of person do you want to be?" After I told him, he asked, "What can I do to help you get there? What can I pray for?"

He didn't judge me; he genuinely cared and showed it by the way he related to me. The more accepting he became, the more I trusted him. Accountability became a safe place for me to share my secrets.

It didn't take long for John to share his messy life with me, and before I knew it, we were two guys in the same boat trying to navigate the same river. Only now, we had two guys with oars paddling together.

John invested his time and compassion. He cared enough to ask about my life. When he nudged me, I could dodge the questions or I could open up. As I learned to trust, I realized that his questions demonstrated his concern. John gave me the confidence to shine a light on the monsters inside my closet.

His response to my answers also increased my self-confidence. When I confessed my deepest problems, he replied with two magic words: "I understand."

Just to hear those two words made my spirits soar. *I wasn't alone in my struggle. He gets it.* His light penetrated into the deepest recesses of my closet, saw the most awful things lurking there, and cast out the darkness with those two words, "I understand."

Concern and empathy create trust. With trust comes freedom, and with freedom eventually comes healing. That's God at work. That's the power of accountability.

DO I HAVE TO GO BACK AND CONFESS TO THOSE I HURT?

You have to answer that one yourself. Perhaps this true story about "Jessica" and how she faced accountability will help. Jessica had been a believer for five years when she formed an accountability partnership with another friend. Until then, she had lived a fairly happy life.

But before she turned to Christ, she had made many poor choices. For example, she once stole money from her employer, a major retailer. No one caught her. Although she felt guilty over her crime, she pushed aside the lurking, disquieting memory.

After she had been meeting with her accountability partner for several months, Jessica decided to share that secret sin—something she'd never told anyone. "I stole $200," she said.

Her partner didn't judge her. Instead, she asked Jessica how she felt about the theft.

To her own surprise, Jessica talked about feelings of shame for the next few minutes. "I didn't realize how troubled I was over stealing that money." Tears slid down her cheeks.

"My emotions shocked me," she said later, "but the tears didn't last. By the time we walked out of that coffee shop, I was smiling. I felt as if an enormous weight had been lifted off me."

With time, prayer, and support, Jessica worked toward making restitution to the employer. That was her decision; her accountability partner asked one question, "What do you still need to do to be free from that burden?"

"To repay the money," Jessica blurted out. And as she spoke the words, she knew it was the right thing for her to do.

We can draw an important lesson from Jessica's story—secret sins bind us in ways we don't always understand. They're like an invisible anchor. As Jessica confessed her sins during other accountability sessions, more burdens lifted.

Hal handled his situation differently. He and a friend had cheated on an important college exam. "I probably would have passed anyway, but I don't know about my friend." Hal had been out of college twelve years before he became a serious believer.

His accountability partner wisely pushed Hal to make his own decision. "What good would it do now? It's too late to undo the cheating. My friend has a responsible position in a major corporation. It wasn't right to hurt him just to soothe my conscience."

These two accounts also demonstrate that we don't need to confess to the person we've betrayed, cheated, or hurt, at least not at first. Whether God leads us to confess to them, accountability offers a safe place to make the first confession—and to have the freedom of knowing it's no longer hiding inside and tormenting us.

Here's another example: In my ministry, I've counseled many people who've had affairs. They're racked with guilt and shame. They want to repent, but they're afraid if they tell their spouse, the truth will kill their marriage.

I don't tell people they must confess their sins to those they've hurt. God must lead them to that decision. It's a heavy, heavy thing to consider.

Direct confession is such a monumental event that most of us will avoid it. However, accountability offers a middle ground between direct confession and silence—we can unburden ourselves to someone we trust. The accountability relationship can bring peace while the person decides whether it's wise to try to make amends.

DOUBLE-SECRET SINS

Sometimes we hide double-secret sins. By that, I mean not only do we hide a sin from others, but also we hide it from ourselves. It's called *denial*. This may well be what David meant: "How can I know all the sins lurking in my heart? Cleanse me from these hidden [sins]" (Psa. 19:12).

We deny self-knowledge about the behavior and thoughts we want to avoid. We stare at our reflection in the mirror, don't like what we see, and we don't want to look again. As with secrets we keep from others, denial is no way to live. Accountability holds up a mirror and lovingly shows us our true struggles.

For example, we often deny deep-seated anger. We keep it from ourselves. And we try to keep it from God.

My co-writer, Cec Murphey, has participated in several accountability partnerships and groups. One group met every Thursday, including holidays, for four years. During one of the first meetings, Cec shared a bad experience he'd had with a book editor. "He lied to me and persuaded me to agree to an unfair contract," he told the group.

"How'd that make you feel?" Greg asked.

"Hurt," Cec said, "but I've forgiven him."

"No, you haven't."

Shocked, Cec replied, "Sure, I have. I forgave him soon after it happened."

Greg shook his head. "Your voice gives you away. You might want to forgive him, but you're still angry."

As Cec stared at the other man, he considered the inner tension he felt, and the tone of voice he had used when discussing the editor's insults. "You're right," he said. "I'm still angry."

Greg and the other men ministered to Cec after his confession. It took several more days, but the compassion of those men enabled him to truly forgive the editor.

"They didn't condemn me," Cec said. "They loved me enough to confront me with the truth."

Cec learned an important principle: "What I *know* about myself is what I *say* about myself." Until he admitted his anger—saying it aloud—he couldn't know himself or receive healing. In later accountability meetings, Cec discovered other bad feelings he had kept hidden. Only when his partners pointed them out and he acknowledged them, did he finally realize how he felt.

Whether your secret sins are hidden from the world or only from yourself, you suffer from the darkness that conceals them. The darkness entangles you and limits the life you're supposed to live. To experience true freedom, you need to shine a light on what's hidden. Accountability is the ideal way to do just that.

Chapter 4

HOW DO I FIND THE RIGHT PARTNER?

How do I know the right person to choose? How do I know whom I can trust?

There's no easy answer for this question. You begin, of course, by praying for God to lead you to the partner who is right for you. You may not find that person immediately. You may start with the wrong person and need to move out of that relationship (see chapter 11). Be careful. Be sure. But also be bold. This is a mission for your spiritual growth. You don't want to wait to see if God will send you someone.

Trust your instincts. When you meet someone you want to consider, pay close attention to your reactions. "Mac will be the perfect accountability partner," a friend may say. Don't accept that—even if it's correct. As you meet and discuss accountability, if you find yourself holding back or are uncertain, take no action.

You need only say, "Let's leave this for now and both of us will pray about it." That gives you emotional distance to check out your gut reactions.

Talk with several people, especially those who are in a good accountability situation. You might say, "You know the kind of person I am. Do you know anyone you think might become a good partner for me?"

Some of us talked to many individuals before we found exactly the right person. I definitely urge you to choose someone of the same sex. That should seem obvious, but I'll say that it avoids problems of crossing the line from friendship to sexual issues.

We make decisions differently, so I wouldn't want to tell you how to choose. For example, my co-writer makes his best decisions intuitively. This isn't the same as choosing a partner, but here's his experience.

He is a writer, and today most published writers need literary agents. He had been with one agency for more than six years. Agents sell the work of writers and it needs to be a close, trusting relationship. Cec grew increasingly dissatisfied with the relationship and he and his agent parted.

Cec knew a number of agents and considered several. After prayer, he contacted three of them. He emailed each of them and offered to fly to the city where each lived. "I was sure that when I met the right person, I would know," he said. He flew to Ohio and met one agent. "I liked him, but it wasn't quite right."

The second agent had a problem and had to postpone the meeting. He met the third one. "Within three minutes after we met, I knew that was the agent I wanted." Cec has now been with that agency more than a decade. *He knew.*

Others decide by looking at specific criterion. Here's a list of qualities you might consider. That person:

- **is already a friend, or someone you think you would like to know better.**

- **appears to have a strong commitment to God.**

- **is someone you can trust to hold things in confidence.**

- **wants to grow spiritually.**

- **would meet weekly or bi-weekly.**

- **is willing to challenge you and is open to being challenged.**

There may be other qualities. You might ask advice from a few people who are already in committed accountability relationships.

But once you have a clear idea of what you want, you might ask the person to lunch or coffee or to talk after a church meeting.

Below are a few guidelines for things you might say at that meeting.

- "I've asked you to meet with me because I want to grow in my Christian faith. I thought you might help me to grow and I could help you."

- "If you're interested in discussing this, I'd like to tell you what I have I mind."

- "I call this an accountability relationship. I want to make myself answerable to you. In return, I want you to be accountable to me."

- "I've made a list of qualities I'd like to see in an accountability partner. From what I know and have observed about you, I think you fit them. May I read you the list?"

- "I don't know if you're interested in being my accountability partner, but I'd like you to consider it."

When you state exactly what you want to receive and what you have to offer in an accountability partnership, it makes it easier. You lay it out before you start. Make it easy for the other person to accept or to turn down. You don't want that person to feel pushed into a partnership that doesn't fit his or her needs.

You need to ask the questions; you *also need to listen to the answers. If you sense that one or two yellow lights flash*, it's easy to say, "Let's both pray about this." If all the lights turn green, you can proceed.

ONCE YOU CHOOSE

Once you choose a partner, I have a few things to help you get started.

1. The most obvious is to set the date and the time for the initial meeting. How often will you meet? Do you change meetings that conflict with other things? (Cec's group of six that met for four years decided they would meet every Thursday with no interruption, not even holidays such as Thanksgiving. That meeting took priority over everything else. You may not want something with that high level of commitment.)

2. At your first meeting, relax and open yourself to your partner as much as possible. Give your partner equal opportunity. Chances are that one of you will talk more than the other. As in marriage, we tend to relate to those who complete our personality. Some would say opposites, but that's too strong. You also need areas of commonality. Perhaps it will help if we show you how accountability partnerships work.

Cec and Dave have been accountability partners so long neither is quite sure when it began. Dave taught psychology at a local college and Cec was a pastor. After the two met at a seminar, Cec began to recommend people with serious problems to seek Dave's services. Eventually Cec and Dave met for lunch and after that they continued to meet regularly. As they met more frequently and spoke more openly to each other, the relationship deepened. Cec says they didn't use the term until after he made contact with me and realized that he and Dave were accountable.

By nature, Cec is outgoing and exuberant. He's quick to respond. (When Cec was a missionary in Kenya, the Africans called him *Haraka*, which means *quick*.) He's also a risk-taker and willing to try new things.

Dave is quiet, more introspective, and slower to make decisions. He tends to be cautious. When they discuss new actions, Dave often tells Cec, "You're the scout. I'll watch you and then I'll do it."

They constantly and lovingly monitor each other's attitude and actions. "It's easy for me to hear Dave's rebukes," Cec says, "because I know he loves me and wants only the best for me."

3. Like any new relationship, start slowly and be relaxed. Do you like your new partner? Do you feel comfortable with that person? It won't take more than a couple of meetings for you to sense if you can continue.

In my first relationship with John, we started our partnership because we were already friends. That already-established relationship made it easy to connect with him. We met in coffee shops and restaurants, sometimes at his home, and other times at mine. We started by telling the other a few things about ourselves. As we continued to meet, we realized we had several common struggles.

4. Make sure there is the right chemistry. It's present or it isn't. There needs to be a certain amount of trust and respect *for* each other and a reasonably equal amount of neediness *from* each other. Being in an accountability relationship with someone is quite different from being their mentor or mentee. It is vital that you understand the environment of both.

A mentor relationship means that one of you is the teacher and the other is the learner. In accountability partnerships, both are teachers, both are learners. One may be wiser or more experienced, but the relationship thrives because both of you share, teach, and learn from the other.

That's why the chemistry is vital. It's fairly obvious when it's present and easy to know when it is not. Take a look at someone whom you already hang out with and like to fish with, travel, shop, play together, or join in social events. If that person also has the kind of walk with God you admire, you have a great chance of hitting it off.

5. Self-reveal only as much as you're comfortable doing. Whatever secrets you have, I can assure you that you're not unique. I think of the words of Paul who wrote to the Christians at Corinth. (The seaport at Corinth was supposedly one of the busiest sex-trade areas of the ancient world.) He wrote these words of encouragement to them, "The temptations in your life are no different from what others experience. And God is faithful. He will not allow the temptation to be more than you can stand. When you are tempted, he will show you a way out of that so you can escape" (1 Cor. 10:13). That escape route might be your accountability partner.

Over the past fourteen years, I've had ten accountability partners. One of them moved to Canada; another had a schedule change. In two instances, it was time for both of us to move on. I point this out because accountability is usually for a period of time. It's not a lifetime commitment.

For example, Cec speaks of his six-man group that lasted four years until he moved. Jim Martin, another accountability partner, moved out of state after seven years. David Morgan has been Cec's accountability partner at least twenty years. They meet each Tuesday and rarely skip meetings. At one point, Cec moved from Atlanta to Louisville for four years. He and David talked for about an hour by telephone every Saturday. Within a week after Cec's move back to Atlanta, he and Dave met and resumed the relationship.

"Our relationship was too perfect for me to let it go," Cec said. "I've never been able to trust another man the way I've learned to trust Dave. I think he feels the same about me."

WHEN IS A GOOD TIME TO START?

The obvious answer is ASAP. We know there are times when we're much more ready to open up to someone else. Most of us are more open during crisis times in our lives. We don't like the way things are and we're not sure how to change them. Having an accountability partner is a good start.

The men with whom I've interacted have started in the midst of a personal crisis. They finally admitted they couldn't handle everything by themselves and needed someone to whom they could open up and who would correct their thinking. That's the beginning of many accountability partnerships. The down side is that once the crisis is over, sometimes the once-troubled partner decides to move on. "I don't need the relationship any longer," they say.

I think they're wrong, because life is filled with crises and we always, always need someone to guard our back.

GENDER COUNTS

Again, I want to emphasize that you need to make sure the person is the same sex. That choice avoids unwanted complications. Recently I took a call from a husband in distress who wanted marriage counseling and I asked, "What's the issue?"

He enlightened me with a terrible situation where his wife had been spending countless hours helping a man who lived across the street. "The man is recovering from his divorce and she spent as much time there as she did at home."

"Why is she consoling your *male* neighbor?"

"Because I encouraged her to go every night with dinner and help him get through his divorce." He said it had been going on for three months.

"How's that working out for you?"

"She wants a divorce. She wants to marry my neighbor." He broke down and sobbed.

That example alone is reason enough. And I've known other complicated situations with cross-gender accountability. I won't say it never works, but why put yourself in a state of temptation?

Leave that kind of work to the professionals. Even when my wife and I mentor couples together, I'm cautious about how I speak to women. My guard remains high with the opposite sex at all times. When a woman asks me for help, I route her to my wife. If my wife isn't available, I recommend a pastor or counselor.

I encourage you to find someone of the same gender whom you enjoy being with and make sure they are not afraid to challenge you. The accountability process can change your life forever.

DETERMINE THE FREQUENCY

Although mentioned above, it's important to set clear objectives when you begin meeting. Agree to a certain day, time, and location. Loose commitments quickly unravel the accountability process and come to an end.

Meet weekly if your schedules allow. Bi-weekly will work, but it is not the preferred frequency because of busy schedules. It's more difficult for you to keep your time protected when you don't meet weekly.

Another positive reason to meet weekly is the frequent encouragement you receive and offer. Knowing that you will connect on a deep level every week with a non-biased person who cares for you can be extremely comforting.

DETERMINE THE LOCATION

Meeting in a public place such as a coffee shop or a restaurant can be effective. It has been for me; however, Cec prefers privacy, such as a home or in a park.

Not long ago I visited a friend in Nashville. We decided to get up early and go to the local coffee shop for accountability talk. After I walked inside, I spotted four other pairs of men and women doing the same, with mocha in one hand and a Bible in the other.

Another reason I like meeting in public is because it may feel better to get out of the environment of your home and away from the distractions of your family. Be cautious and pick a spot that is not too noisy or distracting.

Cec's reason is exactly the opposite. He and David alternate home visits. They go into a room, close the door, and no one interrupts them. That works for them. Cec says he doesn't want anyone to eavesdrop or to have someone come by to chat at a moment when he and David are in deep conversation.

The important thing is to find a place that is compatible to both of you.

DETERMINE THE QUANTITY

Some people want only one person for a partner. Some have accountability groups of four or five. I highly recommend no more than four as it becomes difficult for everyone to have the time to share and learn to trust each other. The trust factor is primary. Your ability to find so many people that you trust with the right chemistry can be challenging. Confidentiality also is more difficult to maintain with multiple people.

I prefer to have only one partner at a time. As mentioned above, Cec was once part of a group of six. "I don't think it would happen again," he says. "We were six men, all at about the same level of pain and need. It worked for us." He tried a six-man group twice after that and it didn't work.

BE THE LIFELINE

Once you start, here are two things to keep in mind. First, be a *lifeline* for your partner. Determine to give more help than you receive. That is, don't go primarily to get your needs met. Go for the other person. A powerful spiritual rule says it this way: It's in the giving that we receive.

Second, getting an accountability partner is about improving *yourself and your partner.* It's not a gripe session and it's not to rail on about your spouse, boss, co-workers, pastor, or anyone else. The goal is for you to become a godly, victorious Christian.

At times you will share issues about others, but fight the urge to use your time as a dumpsite. Bear in mind that failing in relationships with others is usually a result of poor choices by both parties. Accountability is about you and what you can do for yourself.

You can't heal anyone else. You can't heal the people who have spoken against you or plotted against you. You can learn to understand and to forgive and allow God to bring healing to you.

BEWARE OF FRIENDS

Choosing the right friends is one of the crucial life decisions you make as a Christian. The rule holds true that like attracts like. Look at your friends. Miserable people usually mingle with those who are miserable. If you want to be successful, surround yourself with successful, optimistic individuals. Healthy marriages are usually surrounded by marriages that are healthy.

The people of the first century must have faced the same problems. The apostle Paul warns that "bad company corrupts good character" (1 Cor. 15:33).

Peter writes strongly about false teachers and those who lead others astray: "These people are as useless as dried-up springs or as mist blown away by the wind. They are doomed to blackest darkness. They brag about themselves with empty, foolish boasting. With an appeal to twisted sexual desires, they lure back into sin those who have barely escaped from a lifestyle of deception" (2 Peter 2:17–18).

I was struck by his statement of those who have "barely escaped a lifestyle of deception." (Deception can refer to sin of any kind.) In my old lifestyle, I was ensnared by sinful living. People with whom I associated seemed to enjoy the sinful life that I wanted to escape.

As I prayed about the situation, I realized the only way to find freedom—to escape—was to leave those relationships. Within weeks of my full commitment to Jesus Christ, except for one person, I lost every friend. The one person, who was my best friend, understood my heart and was able to love and support me as I escaped from an immoral, corrupting lifestyle.

What does this say to you? I want it to encourage you to evaluate the friends inside your circle of influence. By what kind of people are you surrounded? Who are the people to whom you listen? What are the values of those you call friends?

Of course, first you need to identify what I've called your circle of influence. By that term, I mean your closest friends or those who impact your decisions. They give advice and you listen. You do the things they do and go where they go.

The closest friends are individuals in your life who significantly impact your thoughts and actions. They are the people to whom you turn when frustrated or excited with good news.

Consider them. If they don't encourage you and support your growth, re-form your circle of influence. Move away from them.

If you are married, take a good look at the couples you hang around with the most. If they aren't striving for the same kind of marriage you want, distance yourself from them. You may need to escape from negative friendships. When we use *escape* with the word *from*, it means to break loose. Or a simple way to say it is to *avoid* such relationships.

This isn't to make you judgmental or become what some call the holier-than-thou person. It doesn't mean you pull away from every non-Christian in your circle. It means you reshape the level of outside influence. Focus on positive, healthy relationships and distance yourself from negative, unhealthy ones.

We want to learn to accept those of different values, but we don't have to let them hold influential positions in our circle.

It's possible for you to be part of *their* circle of influence but for them not to be part of yours. Once you escape their influence, you can be the person to whom they come for advice and for someone just to listen.

I'll put it another way. Once your life is stable and strong in the Lord you can carefully reach out to your unbelieving friends. Take your new boundaries with you and try to love them toward Christ without jeopardizing your own walk with God.

Because of the power of influence, guard against those who encourage you to let down your standards or who say, "Oh, that's not so bad."

My friend Jeff Adams says it like this: "Demand perfection. Settle for excellence." You can attain such levels only if you're surrounded by a quality circle of influence.

FACEBOOK, TWITTER, AND OTHER INTERNET CONNECTIONS

In recent years, we have countless opportunities to allow strangers from around the world to enter our personal world. We trade intimate information; we send photos; we become vulnerable. I think of groups such as MySpace, Facebook, ShoutLife, LinkedIn, and Twitter. Months ago I read that the number of members is in the hundred millions and growing.

In early 2008, *Business Week* magazine referred to the MySpace generation. I mention this because the article shows how eager individuals are to open themselves to someone else. They feel isolated or misunderstood and they throw out the most personal, intimate information for strangers to read. Those strangers—and some are predators—influence the MySpace generation.

The Internet connects people to the moral and the immoral, to the wise and the foolish, the true and the false. This isn't to yell at people not to join such groups; it is only to warn. Be careful. Bad company corrupts good character. And that corruption can come by face-to-face encounters, email, or the Internet.

Here's an example: Sharon went to MySpace and other Web sites. The daughter of a pastor, she had already raised three children and wanted to know what went on in the Internet arena. She was shocked by the text transmitted between the teenagers. They talked about hating their parents, the things they did away from home, and some of their statements were sexually explicit. Each seemed to brag about being more sexually active than the others.

"It horrified me to realize the influence those teenagers have over each other. They shared ideas on how to cause harm to their parents and get even for the rules they were being forced to follow."

If you're a parent, I recommend that you monitor your kids' Internet activity. Do you know who communicates with your kids? What are their morals? What are their boundaries? Are they the kind of accountability partners you want them to have?

Maybe you, an adult, struggle with boundaries. Maybe you're not a teen, but you yearn to connect with someone who is safe—someone who will listen and express compassion.

Many, many adults surf the 'Net for hours a day. They meet people and even invite them to visit their homes. Sometimes they marry those they meet in the virtual world of the Internet. Again: Be careful. Be suspicious. Every life you connect with can build you up or tear you down.

I know instances where marriages have crumbled because of one person who met someone else on the Internet. Don't let your marriage be the next one.

Chapter 5

WHY NOT MY SPOUSE?

"My wife is my best friend," Roger told my co-writer, Cec. "We share everything. We don't need anyone else."

"That's too bad."

"Bad? It's wonderful!"

"Is it? It's too bad your wife must carry all your emotional baggage," Cec said. "It's too bad you don't have a male friend to share your struggles."

"I don't need another man. And my wife doesn't need another female friend."

"Really?" Cec asked. "Does she tell you about her menstrual problems and discuss stretch marks?"

"Well, no, not that."

"So there are things she doesn't share? I bet there are male issues you don't share with her."

Roger thought about that before he nodded. "I guess there are a few things."

"You also need someone who can look at you and your marriage objectively," Cec said. "Your spouse can't do that."

I'm sure Roger could have identified many topics he didn't discuss with his wife. Men censor themselves when talking with their spouses. They keep some topics to themselves—such as past relationships, feelings of vulnerability, and male physical issues. Women also censor themselves when it comes to topics a man might not understand.

God programmed men and women differently. Some things we don't understand. In other areas, such as parenting, finances, and spiritual growth, we might disagree, but we can talk about them. That was Cec's point with Roger. Cec wanted him to understand that no matter how much he loved his wife, she couldn't be an effective accountability partner.

WE CAN'T HANDLE THE TRUTH

It's human nature to react negatively when we learn secrets from our spouse. While mentoring couples, I've witnessed occasions where the revelation of a deep personal struggle or past indiscretion led to turmoil in the relationship.

Once during a counseling session, a woman told her husband she was considering a divorce. She divulged that information in an attempt to save the marriage. Until that session, he'd refused to talk to her about their troubled relationships.

He couldn't handle the news. He left the room in a rage. From then on, he pulled even further away from his wife. He punished her by emotional withholding—which is a common method in a troubled marriage. Unable to handle her secret-thoughts-now-revealed, he gave her the opposite of what she desired. (Despite several attempts to talk to them, they never came back. I don't know the end of their story.)

Another time, a husband struggled with romantic feelings toward another woman in his Sunday school class. He hadn't acted on his feelings, and he knew they were wrong. He wanted to do the right thing. He decided his wife should be the first person to whom he should talk.

His wife reacted as if he'd slept with the woman. Devastated by the emotional betrayal, she treated him like an adulterer. She forced him to sever the relationship by leaving that church. "I don't think I can ever trust you again," she said.

I don't want to say she was correct or that she handled it badly. My point is that I think he was unwise to tell her. Another man could have understood and offered him sympathy and guidance.

Many women react with demonstrative emotion, including anger, when faced with a hurtful secret. Many men withdraw and refuse to give their wives the emotional engagement they need. Of course, sometimes the roles are reversed. Both spouses are capable of responding in ways that exacerbate the emotional pain.

Most of us start marriages with high expectations of our spouses. We push them to be who we want them to be. And we censor ourselves in an attempt to be who they want us to be. It's not an environment that promotes absolute truth.

So what's the alternative? If we can't discuss everything with our spouse, should we respect our union by suppressing our struggles and not telling *anyone*? Certainly not.

Within a marriage, those who harbor a secret can reach a point where the pressure grows so intense that they unload their burden thoughtlessly. Desperate for relief, they ignore the potential consequences of their disclosure. Afterward, they might feel relief, even peace, but what about their spouses? How does that affect them? What do they feel?

A healthy marriage needs a safe place to lighten our souls from our burdens. Meeting with a friend for accountability eliminates the emotional harm that can come from divulging our secrets. An accountability partner can provide immediate encouragement and empathy.

For example, let's say a man discloses to his accountability partner a troubling secret about addiction to pornography. What's the first thing that happens? The accountability partner is drawn toward the man who confesses. "I'm here for you," he says. The friend helps to establish a plan for healing. There's no critical spirit and no anger, judgment, or emotional pain. In a neutral tone, the partner offers understanding and support.

Because of the objectivity, an accountability partner offers a distinct advantage over a spouse.

ACCEPTING CRITICISM

Spouses tend to magnify the emotional impact of the words they receive from each other. Unlike anyone else, a spouse can make the other person feel like the best person in the world; but a spouse also possesses the unique ability to make the mate feel worthless.

Too often, when we hear words of rebuke from a mate, we feel the need to protect and to defend ourselves. Attack becomes a strong weapon of self-defense.

If you're married, your spouse has probably confronted you about habitual behavior that bothered him or her. How did you feel about that conversation? Most healthy marriages eventually work out ways to accept criticism, but it's not easily learned.

Some of the couples I've worked with have experienced situations like this: Janet criticizes Bill for dropping his clothes on the bedroom floor. "Why can't you just put things away?" she asks.

Bill, feeling attacked by his wife, retaliates. He doesn't defend his actions (there is no adequate defense) and instead he attacks. "If you kept the kitchen clean, I might be more motivated to pick up around the bedroom."

The battle starts. Unless something intervenes, the fighting escalates. Maybe they yell. Each one fires a response that's stronger than the one just received. Later, they probably forgive each other, but they probably won't forget the anger.

Suppose, however, a friend talked to you about one of your habits. Suppose he talked—unemotionally—to you about the mess in your car. How would you react? I hope you'd thank your friend for the honest feedback. But even if you felt defensive, you probably wouldn't retaliate the way you might with your spouse.

From personal experience, I admit that when the truth came from Pam, the truth seemed harsh. I realized that I accept rebuke and criticism much easier from my accountability partner.

From the Bible we can see that spouses have a distinct purpose in our lives. Marriage is the joining of two equals. "...A man... is joined to his wife, and the two are united into one" (Gen. 2:24).

God created marriage because the first human, Adam, needed a helper and a companion. (See Gen. 2:20.) Many couples don't understand the helper concept, and they wonder why there's so much turmoil in their relationship.

Your job within a marriage is to *help*. That means to love, respect, support, and honor. The job isn't to criticize. Both of you get enough of that outside the marriage. As half of a whole, criticism from a spouse feels like a self-inflicted wound. It hurts deeper, but friends outside the union can say the same things without our feeling such pain. They're not half of who we are.

In accountability, I ask my partner to challenge me in my faith. He can confront me and encourage me to grow. He pushes me deeper and faster to the Lord. I need him to be brutally honest.

A wife who frequently confronts and challenges her husband spiritually will probably come across as self-righteous; however, if she loves and encourages him on his path, his faith will mature through her support. As she continues to grow through the guidance of her church and accountability partner, he'll benefit from the impact of her faith.

COMMUNICATION

While reading the newspaper, a husband stumbled across an article that summarized a scientific study. The headline read: "Women use 20,000 words every day, but men only use 10,000."

The husband waited for his wife to get off the phone, and then showed her the article. "I told you! Wives talk too much."

She glanced at the article. "Sure, it makes sense. We have to repeat everything."

To which the husband replied, "What?"

You might have already heard that joke, but it points out an obvious truth—husbands and wives communicate differently. They have different verbal skills and needs.

Many women tell me, "I can't get my husband to open up. He keeps all his thoughts and emotions buried inside." I also hear that from a few men, but it's usually the husband who retreats from healthy communication. Many men are experts at withholding information and feelings. To self-reveal doesn't come naturally. If he's had a tough day at work, he wants to leave those problems behind when he gets home.

I have a friend, whom I'll call Dale. He gets home from work about half an hour before his wife. He watches as she parks in the driveway and notices how she walks. By observing the way she walks, he has a strong sense of whether he can talk openly. Or he has to retreat in silence because she's had a bad day at the office and will blow up over anything that sounds critical.

As loving helpers, women generally take that silence personally. They suffer from the lack of communication.

When women discuss their husband's communication problems, I tell them to urge their husband to establish an accountability partnership with a godly man. That way, she can be sure he's talking with someone who can encourage him as well as offer constructive criticism. Through accountability, he'll grow accustomed to sharing his thoughts and feelings.

Communication doesn't seem so daunting once an accountability partnership gets him used to the idea. In fact, his partner can hold him accountable for improving his efforts at verbal communication with his wife.

As much as men are experts at withholding information, some women can be experts at sharing it. They often need to vent and communicate their frustrations. Sometimes, however, they're unaware of the consequences. As loving helpers, husbands take their spouse's struggles personally. The negative energy creates a strain on their marriage.

When a man discusses his wife's enthusiasm for communication, I tell him to urge her to establish an accountability partnership with a godly woman. His wife will receive the benefit of objective encouragement and criticism. Accountability will also give her a safe place to share those thoughts and feelings. Back at home, with some of the pressure off, she can choose how much to share.

THE RIGHT PERSPECTIVE

While they support us, accountability partners can also help protect our marriage. With an objective perspective, they help us calm down before disagreements get out of control. Our accountability partners can hold us responsible *for how we behave* in a disagreement. They can also help us identify our spouse's perspective.

For example, a family friend named Debbie had to make a job change that cut her income by two-thirds. Her husband supported the job change. When she talked to other people about it, she mentioned their financial struggle and how they had to cut back in many areas.

Debbie's accountability partner asked her, "How does all this public talk about cutting back affect your husband?"

Debbie thought about it and realized her husband grew quiet whenever she brought it up. "By discussing it, I've made him feel inadequate as a provider, haven't I?"

The accountability partner grasped something that Debbie hadn't seen. Probably she was too close to the situation. The problem with perspective even applies when there is no current strife or conflict.

In summary: God intended our spouses to become one with us in our commitment and service to God. God doesn't call them to be our accountability partners.

WHY I OPPOSE HAVING A PERSON OF THE OPPOSITE SEX AS YOUR PARTNER

Working in the marriage mentoring arena for years has offered me a profound view of relationships that often end because of infidelity. The interesting thing about every case is that infidelity was the *end result* not the *cause*. As we backtracked, we found numerous *warning signs* that included a bright flashing light with a very loud siren going off.

IT BECAME A WARNING:

Your marriage is in danger.

You're going to destroy your marriage.

You're taking a detour away from righteousness.

If only those men or women had an accountability partner, that could have helped them miles up the road from the intersection of infidelity.

I know several people who have friends of the opposite gender. I certainly don't think that's impossible. I do think that when you choose someone of the opposite sex to be your accountability partner, you're opening yourself to trouble.

"He listens to me."

"She cares about me."

"The more I talk to him, the more I wonder if I'm married to the right person."

"If you really loved me, you'd treat me the way she does."

Those things happen. It's foolish to see how close you can come to another car on the road without hitting it. Isn't it more sensible to stay a safe distance from the other vehicle?

Chapter 6

SEXUAL PURITY

Some people don't like the term, *sexual purity*. "It sounds restrictive," they say. That's true.

"It sounds legalistic." Maybe.

I also know that most couples are already sleeping together before they marry. It's acceptable to society; few people seem shocked to learn that a man and a woman have been together two years before they decide to get married.

Socially acceptable or not, sexual purity is the biblical standard for those who want a healthy marriage relationship.

If you are one of those who didn't postpone sexual gratification until marriage, you can't undo the fact. You can confess to God and ask forgiveness for starting your marriage wrong.

I want to be honest with you about my life. For years accountability partners helped me wrestle with some of the temptations (and actual sin) in my life. Progress was always present but complete victory wasn't. Like thousands, if not millions, of men in America, I struggled with lust. I struggled as a teenager, and even to this day it is the one thing that I must continually cast down at the foot of the cross.

As I mentioned earlier, my accountability partners helped me stay away from sexual relationships with women while I was single and in my late twenties. My accountability to them helped me pave the way for almost six years of purity that led me to the joyous event of matrimony.

My wife and I enjoyed the physical fruits of love, post-marriage. One of the most romantic ways to enter into the sanctity of marriage is when two people refrain from sexual activity and discover that part of their love together after the wedding.

Love is never about self; it's always about the other person. That's the first and most important lesson I learned by remaining sexually pure. It wasn't merely not doing something or refraining from doing, but it was preparing for a special period of my life. By remaining sexually pure, I was ready to give myself fully and totally to *the* woman in my life. I've never regretted it. Not only do I believe I honored God, but I know my wife, Pam, is one of the godliest women I could have ever dreamed of marrying—a true gift from the Lord.

WHERE IT BEGAN

It doesn't matter where your failures begin, but it does matter where they go. For me, pornography is where it began. Even now, it burdens my heart to think of how far from God porn is and the journey it takes us on. I was a Christian, a warrior, a leader, in the ministry, in a high-level position with a prestigious company. Outwardly I had everything a single man could want. But no one knew of my deep inner struggles. Some therapists contend that porn is a symptom of deeper needs and the porn becomes the balm—the pain killer—for deeper needs.

They may be right. I wasn't aware of deeper needs, but I was aware of the addictive nature of pornography. At first I watched a skin flick—a short one—or I went to a Web site "just to see what they have there." Within a year, I realized I was addicted to porn.

"Research indicates that even non-sex addicts will show brain readings on PET scans while viewing pornography similar to cocaine addicts looking at images of people taking cocaine. This material is potent, addictive and permanently implanted in the brain."[2]

Since scientists have shown the immense negative impact, we need to acknowledge how it threatens the family unit. I went through different modes of confession with my accountability partners and different stretches between victory and failure.

After Pam and I married, we enjoyed the newness of our relationship and I valued the intimacy in our first few years. My struggles with lust I kept hidden behind the dark screen on my computer.

Pam and I had been honest with each other about our pasts and we both entered into marriage with no secrets. She knew about my past struggles with porn, but she didn't know that the temptation had slowly crept back into my life. "Just an occasional porn site," I told myself. "It's nothing serious—not like before." I was lying to myself, or trying to, and I said nothing to Pam.

THE NIGHT IT ALL CAME OUT

Pam had dressed and we were ready to go on our regular Friday night date. That weekly date was important to both of us as we tried to protect the time from friends and family and reserve it for the two of us.

"Honey, were you looking at something inappropriate on the computer?"

I froze. I felt blood pump through my body at the speed of sound, and I started to get a little light headed. Like most people who are caught unexpectedly, I began with a lie. "No, why do you ask?"

"A few minutes ago I wanted to search for information on the Web I had looked at yesterday. I clicked on Internet Explorer and up popped pornographic material."

As she spoke, I realized I had not closed off the site, only left it on the bottom of the screen.

"That is odd," I said. I walked across the room to get my keys so we could go out. I couldn't look directly at her. But I couldn't stand the deceit. I felt as if I had compounded my sin by lying or deceiving her.

With my heart pounding I walked over to her. "Sit down. I need to say something." I confessed two things. One was that I lied. Two was that I was guilty of looking at porn—both confessions difficult to say to the person I loved most in my life.

At first she said nothing—I think it was the shock. Tears formed in her eyes and slid down her cheeks. She wiped her eyes and told me she was hurt that I had gone back into porn. She was angry that I had let it happen and said nothing to her.

I felt as if I deserved the worst punishment possible. *Will she leave me? Want a divorce? Hate me?*

After a short time, she said, "Let's go."

"Go where?" I deserved being sent to a firing squad.

"Let's go on our date." She looked into my eyes and said, "I don't understand your struggle with lust, and what you did hurts me deeply, but I love you."

I wasn't prepared for such mercy and hardly knew what to say.

"My role as your wife is to help you and that is what I intend to do."

I cried. I wept right there as I stared at her.

We finally went out, but fresh tears came while we were at the restaurant. On the drive home, more tears fell.

Her compassion made me know I could beat the temptation that constantly tugged at me. Just to talk to her about it made the battle easier.

Not every wife will respond with mercy and love as Pam did. But if you're a woman reading this, I urge you to extend mercy. It may not be easy, but it's possible. Your marriage began with the vow to love and honor "in sickness or in health." His may not be a physical sickness, but it is a sickness.

I want to remind you of a few verses in the Bible—not to slap you in the face but to remind you of the way God works in our lives. Jesus said, "God blesses those who are merciful, for they have shown mercy" (Matt. 5:7).

Don't overlook what we call the golden rule, which are words spoken by Jesus—words commanded by him. "Do to others whatever you would like them to do to you. This is the essence of all that is taught in the law and the prophets" (Matt. 7:12).

And one more word from the Lord: "Do not judge others, and you will not be judged. For you will be treated as you treat others. The standard you use in judging is the standard by which you will be judged" (Matt. 7:1-2).

You may not be guilty of the same sin as your husband, but you're human and you fail. What do you expect him to do if you fail? Paul reminds us, "If you think you are standing strong, be careful not to fall" (1 Cor. 10:12). His point is that none of us is so strong, so pure, and so committed that we won't stumble if the right temptation comes along.

If you're a man reading this, I give you the same advice. In recent years I hear more and more stories of the infidelity of wives. I've heard there are porn sites and magazines for them. In today's culture they face some of the same issues.

Regardless of your gender, you can offer mercy, forgiveness, and understanding to your spouse.

MERCY NOT MALICE

Pam showed me mercy, which I didn't deserve. But isn't that the definition of mercy? and of grace? and of love? None of those are earned or deserved. When Pam forgave me, she did many powerful things to make our marriage stronger. Most of all, I've never wanted to be more pure than I felt the need for at that moment. Her *reaction* stimulated a *passion* in me to conquer my battle more than anything I could have scripted.

My secret was out and Satan's bondage was broken. My wife had entered the game and didn't watch from the sideline. She stood by my side and became a true helper in the biblical sense. Before God created Eve, he said, "I will make a helper who is just right for [Adam]" (Gen. 11:18b).

GET IN THE GAME

The odds of your mate winning the battle of lust go up when you choose to join in the fight. I never said it would be easy, just necessary. Never forget that your sin is no prettier to God than your spouse's.

I wonder if you've ever noticed the list of sins in the New Testament. For instance, Paul lists a number of sins: "...Their lives became full of every kind of wickedness, sin, greed, hate, envy, murder, quarreling, deception, malicious behavior and gossip. They are backstabbers, haters of God, insolent, proud and boastful" (Rom. 1:29–30). Read that list and notice that gossip, quarreling, and backstabbing are in the same list as murder. It seems as if God doesn't deal with degrees of sin, but only recognizes wrong behavior and urges us to flee from anything that holds us back from godliness.

Regardless of the failure of your mate, choose to go down the road of forgiveness and mercy. Embrace the fact that we've all sinned and fallen short of the glory of God (Rom 3:23). The wages of sin is death, which we all deserve equally, husbands and wives, parents and children. *All* includes you, but God gives us an unearned gift of forgiveness and eternal life.

My best is still billions of miles away from the righteousness of God and the righteousness of my wife is as well. Wives, find a way to give your husband mercy; husbands, find a way to give your wife mercy. My wife chose not to crucify me and that choice was one that led me to victory. Please wrap this thought around you and let it sink into the core of your spirit as you strive to be the best spouse you can be.

Exposure for me wasn't easy, but it was necessary for me to find victory. If we can expose our secrets we can begin the process of healing and triumph. Many of us cannot start by sharing our secrets with our spouse. That is the reason why having an accountability partner is so crucial. We need an outlet, a safe place, somewhere for the truth to take hold onto our life.

A FINAL WORD ON THIS

For more resources that can help you gain freedom from pornography, go to any of the following Web sites:

- **www.settingcaptivesfree.com**

- **www.covenanteyes.com**

- **www.accountable2you.com**

Chapter 7

LOVING REBUKE

We don't like the word *rebuke*. We remember our parents' tongue-lashings and how terrible they made us feel. But as children, we needed such admonition in addition to affirmation and encouragement. We needed constructive criticism to learn how to live proper lives. Adulthood doesn't give us perfect knowledge. As children of God, we still need to be corrected and challenged with the truth.

The Bible mentions rebuke more than one hundred times. Here are five different instances:

"ANYONE WHO REBUKES A MOCKER WILL GET AN INSULT IN TURN...BUT CORRECT THE WISE AND THEY WILL LOVE YOU. INSTRUCT THE WISE AND THEY WILL BE EVEN WISER" (PROV. 9:7A, 8B).

"AN OPEN REBUKE IS BETTER THAN HIDDEN LOVE! WOUNDS FROM A SINCERE FRIEND ARE BETTER THAN MANY KISSES FROM AN ENEMY" (PROV. 27:5-6).

"PATIENTLY CORRECT, REBUKE, AND ENCOURAGE YOUR PEOPLE WITH GOOD TEACHING" (2 TIM. 4:2B).

"...DO NOT MAKE LIGHT OF THE LORD'S DISCIPLINE, AND DO NOT LOSE HEART WHEN HE REBUKES YOU, BECAUSE THE LORD DISCIPLINES THOSE HE LOVES, AND PUNISHES EVERYONE HE ACCEPTS AS A SON" (HEB. 12:5 NIV).

"THOSE WHOM I LOVE I REBUKE AND DISCIPLINE..." (REV. 3:19 NIV).

In 2 Samuel, we read the story of King David's adultery and the murder he ordered to disguise his sin. His actions angered God, who sent the prophet Nathan to confront David. Nathan told David a story about a rich man whose actions mirrored David's. When David heard the story, the rich man's behavior enraged him, and he declared, "The man who did this deserves to die!"

Then Nathan confronted David and announced, "You are that man!" (2 Sam. 12:7).

The biblical examples are many. Moses rebuked the Israelites. Jesus rebuked Peter, the father of the Christian church (Matt.17:23).

If David and Peter needed to be confronted when they went astray, doesn't that make it clear that we do also? It's not the issue of the *severity* of the wrongdoing, but the *fact* of the wrongdoing.

An accountability program offers a safe place for confrontation. Meeting one-on-one or in a small group with our peers, an accountability program can lovingly challenge you without the scolding you might have received as a child.

In today's supersensitive, politically correct society, too many don't want to offend anyone. "Who am I to judge?" they ask. To give rebuke feels like unacceptable behavior; to receive rebuke feels like inviting disrespect.

To avoid compassionate confrontation isn't biblical. And it's certainly not healthy. Think about it: When you overeat or eat unhealthful food, your body responds in a way that makes you uncomfortable and reminds you of your poor choices. In the same way, when you make bad actions, you need the body of Christ (those godly people in your life) to remind you of the way to live the better life.

If you want to grow and accomplish great things, you need to learn to accept rebuke. Here's my philosophy on the healthy Christian life: *The same degree that you allow yourself to be held accountable by a trusted friend is the degree to which you'll lead a spiritually successful life.*

With an accountability partner, the idea is simple: If you love me, you'll look out for me and confront the self-destructive areas of my life. I will do the same for you.

My current accountability partner has confronted me many times. Through that confrontation, I've experienced a deeper love for people and a healthier sense of humility. It has helped me to see the areas where I was blind.

The most important rebuke I ever received occurred during my struggle with my ex-girlfriend. I committed my life to Christ after I had broken up with her. I couldn't stay committed to God while I pursued my carnal desires for her. But she tried to work her way back into my life.

During that time, I met John Rios, whom I've already mentioned. We both played on my church softball team and almost immediately we became good friends. During one particular game, my personal problems distracted me, and I couldn't concentrate on the game.

John sensed something was wrong. "What's bothering you?" he asked.

I decided to tell John about my struggles.

"Would you like to become my accountability partner?" he asked.

With trepidation, I said yes, although I didn't understand what it entailed. I just knew I had hit bottom on my own and needed help.

We met regularly. John told me to call him, day or night, if I ever had a weak moment, and he would pray with me. That worked. Several times I called. One evening, however, I didn't call. That's when my former girlfriend phoned me. It was a serious mistake. Maybe I didn't contact John because, deep inside, I knew it was wrong for me to talk to her.

Even worse than talking on the phone, after a long discussion, I agreed that she could come over to my place. We would "just talk." But, of course, we didn't just talk. One thing led to another, and I sinned once again. I was devastated. Spiritually destroyed.

I broke my promises to God and to John. I'm going to end up right back where I've always been. In much anguish, I cried out to God to forgive me. I knew I was forgiven; I also knew I would fall again unless I got help.

The next day, with a shaking hand and pounding heart, I dialed John's number. I blurted out what happened.

"Meet me at Burger King in fifteen minutes," he said. By the time I arrived, John was already seated in a booth. I sat down and hung my head. Tears filled my eyes.

As my accountability partner, he lovingly and firmly let me have it. "I'm disappointed you didn't let me help you," he said. "What happened to our plan? You agreed to call me when you faced trouble." He reminded me that I had promised to contact him during my times of temptation and he would do the same.

I broke down and really cried. I buried my head in my hands. My body shook. "Please forgive me," I said through my sobs.

"I'm going to continue to walk with you, but you need to take our accountability seriously; otherwise, it's simply a waste of time."

Together we prayed, and I asked God to forgive me.

When we finished talking, we hugged, and John walked out of Burger King with me—his arm wrapped around my shoulder like a compatriot helping an injured soldier off the battlefield.

After that, I remained celibate until the day I married my wife five years later. Through accountability with John, God sowed the threads of my aimless life into a life committed to him. The whole course of my life was altered. For the first time I had direction, strength, and momentum. Accountability with John changed everything. I met Pam at my church; I studied the Bible; I eventually went into full-time ministry.

Loving rebuke can save a life; I know that from experience.

John eventually moved to Canada, but since then, I've always had an accountability partner. I've had someone to share my challenges —no matter how small or great. I don't want to go through life without someone guarding my back.

For the past fifteen years, I've worked with more than a thousand people in ministry settings: a ministry for sexually abused boys; a singles ministry; and a marriage-mentoring ministry. In each setting, I've encouraged people in their walk with God. Those experiences have taught me that everyone needs to be answerable to someone. Their situations varied, but the human needs are the same.

The following chapters will show you how to begin an accountability partnership and how to keep it going. With accountability and God's guidance, you'll be able to answer the question: Who's got my back?

Chapter 8

TAKE THE D.A.R.E.

Getting to our destination can be challenging when it comes to accountability. Maybe you have tried to develop some form of accountability but you didn't have a road map to follow.

As in most adventures, it's always good to have a guide or a map to help us stay on course. The stereotype says that real men don't ever ask for a map or for directions. I suppose there are enough men like that, but some of us aren't naïve or dumb enough to think we can find our way totally on our own.

Who needs a map? I do. Trust me, I am just as much a pioneer as the next guy and I've tried a few adventures without a map or a compass, but in a couple of hours I found myself right back where I started. By then I was even more confused and I was tired.

D.A.R.E. CAN HELP YOU STAY ON TRACK

I've worked out an acrostic using the word *DARE*, which is easy to remember and I've found helpful. Others have shared positive experiences with me. Even if you don't like having a map, please consider this anyway:

Discover each other's history.

Ask tough questions.

Require action from each other.

Evaluate the progress.

Now I want to explain exactly what I mean by those four items.

DISCOVER EACH OTHER'S HISTORY

Discovering each other's background seems obvious and perhaps looks easy to do. It's not. It's one of the most difficult things to accomplish. As honest as we want to be, we still hold back, especially until we've learned to trust. We unconsciously throw obstacles in the way to keep us safe from too quick or too deep a self-disclosure. That's one reason most conversations stay on a surface level.

In Cec's words, "You don't vomit all over each other," but as you learn to trust the other person, you reveal more. If you're afraid to make yourself vulnerable to a new partner, say it. (Even that's being vulnerable.) For instance, you might say, "I'm emotionally fragile." If that's too wimpy-sentimental for you, try something simple such as, "I don't know how to trust another person. Give me time."

In the six-man group Cec belonged to, at their first meeting, Greg said, "I don't know how to trust other men. When I have, they've taken advantage of me." And it took five or six meetings before Greg was able to open up to us. Within a few months he was able to be as free and vulnerable as the others. "I've learned to trust you," he said.

Too many of us hold back because we may be afraid that people won't like us if they know who we really are. Haven't we heard people say, "If they really knew how I felt..."? Cec's answer to that goes like this, "I would rather be disliked for who I am than to be admired for who I'm not."

A simple-but-powerful tool to help both of you explore and understand the background of the other is to pray together. True prayer is honest prayer. As both of you open yourselves in prayer to God, you're also opening yourselves to each other.

I like to open and close our sessions with prayer—and by that I mean praying aloud. That may be difficult for some people, but I urge them to try anyway. Sincere prayer comes from deep within us and says what we think is important. For me, prayer is a reminder that not only am I opening myself up to God, but in God's presence I become more transparent to my accountability partner.

Initially you may need to tell them your request. The level at which you enter is a signal to them. If you keep your requests generic (good health, closer relationship to God), you encourage the other to take the same route. But suppose you said, "My temper is my biggest problem. Little things set me off and I need help."

What's the message you're giving your new partner? You've opened a door; you've invited that person into your inner psyche or your heart. Your partner may not be that open, but you have shown the way.

Once you've given your request, ask, "How may I pray for you?" The answer you receive may be superficial (and safe) and that's all right. You need to accept your new partner at his or her level and neither of you wants to be gullible.

Pray aloud for each other and petition the Lord on behalf of each other. Investing in this process can bring life-changing rewards. As you become more committed and trusting, you'll have a strong sense of how to pray for each other.

Share each other's goals and determine what each of you wants to accomplish, and set a date that's feasible for both of you. Think of short-term and long-term goals. What do you want to see happen in one month? What do you want to see happen in a year? in ten years? Discuss your aspirations spiritually, financially, relationally, and physically.

I encourage people to start with the little stuff and work up to the bigger issues. For example, start with simple direct things like this:

- **In one week I want to lose three pounds.**

- **I want to go one month without gossiping.**

- **I want to pay off one credit card in three months.**

- **I want to read my Bible every day for five minutes.**

- **I want to grow spiritually.**

- **I have been struggling with my spouse's temper and I want to accept him as he is.**

- **I have been feeling depressed lately and don't know what to do.**

ASK TOUGH QUESTIONS

To ask tough, probing questions may be one of the most underrated tools to use in accountability or friendships.

That doesn't mean the questions will be easy to answer. They're not supposed to be easy, only honest. This may be the first adult who's ever cared enough to push you to examine your thoughts and attitudes.

David says, "Let the godly strike me! It will be a kindness! If they correct me, it is soothing medicine. Don't let me refuse it" (Psa. 141:5). Or the wise man states, "Wounds from a sincere friend are better than many kisses from an enemy" (Prov. 27:6).

Asking questions can be a powerful way to tell someone you care. It says you care too much to let the other person make unwise choices or to go astray. Years ago I read a book called *Caring Enough to Confront*. I don't remember anything about the book except the title. That's where tough questions originate.

I want to be clear here. The questions aren't meant for me to push anyone to make the decision I think the person ought to make. The purpose is to help the accountability partner face reality in order to make the right decision.

Tough questions can be remarkably simple. If you decide on a course of action you might ask things like this:

- **In what areas have you been struggling lately? How often?**

- **How can I help you reach your goals?**

- **How is sin threatening your life?**

- **To what extent are you willing to go in order to acquire victory?**

- **How can I hold you accountable?**

- **What do you want me to do if you continue to fail?**

Here are a few other questions for you to consider:

- **How will your decision affect your relationship with that person?**

- **Do you want her to know how you feel, or do you want to show her she's wrong?**

- **If you confront the person who wronged you, what do you want to happen?**

- **What expectations do you have for the other person's response to you?**

- **If you do that, how will you feel afterward?**

None of the questions above are judgmental. They're not directive and they don't point you to a course of action. They do, however, push you to think about your decision.

Just a note: Accountability meetings should focus on the others in the group and not just you. You're there to receive, but so are they, so focus on them first. Caring about their journey, asking, probing, and dissecting their life is your job. If done right, you'll get your turn.

If you are with a partner who seems unwilling or unable to ask you tough questions, I suggest you nudge and probe about that issue. If the person absolutely won't ask the tough questions, it's not accountability. That person is failing in his or her part of the agreement. (See chapter 11 about how to get out of the partnership.)

Good questions pave the way for life change. Practice this idea, become skillful with questions, and you will be amazed at how they can navigate you through the roughest waters with great success.

Require Action

It's critical to get to the "So what?" of each session. The easy way is to ask, "So what are you going to do about it?" That's usually only the beginning. You can follow up with:

- How often will you do that?

- When will you begin? (As much as possible, insist on a definite time.)

- If you're not ready for this step, what will it take for you to be ready?

- How can I help you not only to take that first step but to stay with you as you take further steps? (This may seem obvious, but it reassures that you're willing to walk beside your partner in making the change.)

Without action, this program is nothing more than a tea party. Or as one friend put it, you move the mud from one spot to the other with no clean-up taking place.

Ask more questions such as:

- How can I pray for you?

- What specifically do you want me to ask God on your behalf?

- How long do you expect this will take you?

- What do you want me to do if there is no improvement in this area in the next ___ weeks?

Requiring action is critically important and could be the one thing standing in the way of marriages being restored, addictions being conquered, hearts being healed, and lives being changed. Repenting is good; but like John the Baptist cried out, "Prove by the way you live that you have repented of your sins and turned to God" (Matt.3:8).

Challenge each other. Give each other assignments that will promote growth in the areas indicated. Be creative and enjoy this step. It's fun to think up ideas that will yield fruit in each other's lives.

I once challenged a husband to surprise his wife with flowers and do his best to fill his role as a loving husband. Their marriage had gone through a rough time and both of them held resentment toward the other. He finally decided to take my challenge. The flowers weren't the point, and he understood. I challenged him to find a way to express love without words.

A few weeks later I ran into his wife and she was so happy to see me. She said, "I don't know what you guys are doing, but whatever it is, keep it up." (He brought her flowers; he listened when she talked to him; he tried to understand her perspective. Best of all, he took her in his arms and said, "Please forgive me." Once he changed, she also changed.)

EVALUATE THE PROGRESS

You need constantly to evaluate the relationship for any plan to stay on track. Before you talk to the other person, I urge you to ask yourself questions such as:

- **How is the relationship growing?**

- **Am I holding back?**

- **Are we moving forward?**

- **Are we making enough progress to consider it worthwhile?**

A common complaint I hear is, "He's a nice guy, but we're not accomplishing anything."

Ask questions of yourself but also ask your partner. Think of it this way: if you feel you're not making progress, your partner may feel the same way. I don't have any particular order, but the following questions focus on areas that often need to be examined:

- **Is our accountability working?**

- **What do you need for me to do to make it better?**

- **What do you need to do to make it better?**

- **Are you giving all that you can? Are you receiving all you can?**

- **Are you being fully honest?**

- **Do you feel as if your partner is measuring up?**

Deal with these questions immediately. Don't ask once, but come back to the questions as often as you need to do so. Plan to do a regular check-up on yourselves. Frequently gauge the temperature of the relationship. Give your accountability a few months to prove it is a good match. Address the concerns and continue to communicate what you want out of it.

Here's a made-up illustration, but I think it makes the point. For two years, Dan and Scott met weekly. By the end of the second year, Dan thought the relationship had grown stagnant. Dan was a little uneasy about addressing his feelings about it, but he decided to speak up. "Hey Scott, how do you think our meetings have been going lately?"

Scott smiled and said, "I'm glad you asked. It's not exciting like it was at first. It's same-old same-old each time."

Through a short conversation they decided to redirect their meetings and begin challenging each other to learn more about what it meant to be baptized as well as what it meant to be a church member. They discussed how theological issues such as baptism affected their relationship with God and with others. Each week they agreed to study separately then come together and share their thoughts and findings. They became excited about meeting again.

Sometimes calling for time out is healthy and gives you confidence that you are meeting with the right person but you need to pull back so you can refocus. When you try various methods and discover that none of them works for you, it may be time to get out of the relationship.

But don't give up; find another partner. It's your future that could be at stake. Here's the thought to keep in mind: If people aren't changing because of their accountability meetings, their meetings are a waste of time.

I know two guys who met for a couple of years. One was a therapist and one was a corporate executive. The therapist felt the executive was becoming too dependent on him and stopped meeting. After seven months, the therapist called the executive again. He had realized two things. First, it wasn't that the businessman was becoming dependent, it was that the therapist himself was fearful of opening up more. His role was to help others trust and become transparent. He could help others, but he didn't know how to do it himself.

When the therapist explained that (and even the explanation was the beginning of his transparency), he said, "I miss you. I'm uncomfortable at times when we're together, but I have no one in my life who pushes me to look at myself the way you do."

That happened several years ago and they continue to meet weekly.

WHAT IF?

Imagine for a moment that Christians across the nation held weekly accountability meetings. What if they allowed God into this process and got serious about their lives? In some ways, that could become far more impacting than any religious program, church, or parachurch ministry could offer. I am all for the church and the services it provides; however, in my opinion, in homes and in the marketplace is where real life change happens. If you are meeting with someone for accountability and that person doesn't D.A.R.E about you, I suggest you find someone who does.

I have met hundreds of individuals who have no intentional accountability in their lives. Just like me fifteen years ago, they think that church on the weekends, occasional praying and Bible reading, along with small talk with their spouses is enough. When their little secrets weighed five ounces they didn't do anything to deal with them. By the time they're desperate for help, those secrets seem to weigh five hundred pounds and are still adding weight. Eventually, the secrets can destroy the people who hold them inside.

I look back and wish I had exposed my secrets and trusted people when the problems weighed only five ounces or even five pounds. They're still manageable then. By the time they become huge weights in our lives, we may have lost our job, our marriage, or turned to some form of addiction as an attempt to deaden our pain.

FINAL THOUGHTS ABOUT D.A.R.E.

This method of communicating works in many arenas besides accountability. I have found it to be an effective method of evangelizing the gospel of Jesus Christ. Think about the process and how it can be used to witness to people whom you encounter. When you ask a series of well thought-out questions, you are doing more than asking questions. Your questions can create a vision in their minds that probably never existed before.

For example, let's assume I ask the following questions to a non-Christian:

- **How fulfilled is your life?**

- **What are the areas in which you have been struggling for the last ten years?**

- **Have you ever thought about your purpose in this world? If so, what do you think it is?**

- **Do you ever feel like you're missing something?**

- **What do you think about eternity?**

- **What are your thoughts on God?**

- **How do you think you get to heaven?**

Can you see the adaptability of D.A.R.E.? Their answers create a vision of need before you offer any solution. God can use those questions to plow their field and cultivate their soil so that they'll be ready for the seeds you will eventually plant.

As they answer those powerful questions, they also create a vision for their life and their needs. At the right time you could introduce the idea of Jesus being the answer. Questions are the key that unlocks the heart. Questions are the way to show your love to an accountability partner or anyone you are trying to impact.

Chapter 9

LET THEM OFF THE HOOK

I wonder if you have the same fear as others with whom I've spoken. "If I don't confront him (or her) and deliver some kind of sting for the wrong he did, it will only get worse. Bad things will happen." They sometimes pause, shake their heads and say, "She (or he) will never change."

First, you don't know if the person will or won't change. You can't make that decision for your spouse. You can pray for repentance, a change of direction, or divine intervention.

Second, how do you know if it will get worse if you don't punish your spouse? (Punishment can be in words, withholding affection, speaking unkindly, gossiping to others, or a myriad of other ways.)

"I can't just sit back and let that happen," one woman said. "I must let him know that my fury will be on the other side of that choice he made and it will only get hotter."

It's human nature to punish anyone who doesn't live up to our expectations. It doesn't have to be a gross form of sin. It can be as simple as not doing things around the house or being late for appointments.

We think we help them move forward by punishing them. Sometimes we do need to invoke what is called tough love. I hear so much of that from couples, I'd like to talk about the other side: I'd like to talk about letting the person off the hook.

By letting them off the hook, I don't mean ignoring or acting as if those things didn't happen. It means facing our mate squarely and saying, in effect, "I know what you did and I'm hurt by your actions. But I love you. I forgive you." Those words may not come immediately, but if we want to follow the biblical pattern of Christian living, that's our goal, isn't it? "If you forgive those who sin against you, your heavenly Father will forgive you. But if you refuse to forgive others, your Father will not forgive you" (Matt. 6:14-15). Those are the words of Jesus.

When we let our spouses off the hook for their failure and we offer them mercy, the opposite of our fear usually happens. We draw them closer to us and our behavior of mercy can trigger their behavior to change in the direction we want.

I'll give you an example. Years ago Pam and I went fishing with my dad. I had a fishing boat and we went to a small lake in Iowa. The fishing was great and it was just the three of us out there enjoying life. While we were in the middle of the lake, Pam asked me to take her to the shore. She wanted to drive over to the food shack and see what they had. As I pulled up to the bank, I reminded her to be extra cautious when she backed up the truck because of the boat trailer being on the back. When backing up, it was difficult to see it. I reminded her, "It's easy to jackknife and run over the trailer if you're not careful."

She got out and Dad and I went back to fishing. We were about fifty yards off shore and Pam yelled out from the bank, "Matt! Come here! I think there is something wrong with the trailer."

I thought that was odd. It was fine when I parked the truck. I trolled up to the bank as she explained that she thought it was out of alignment. That made no sense to me.

I walked up to the truck and realized what happened. She had accidentally backed up over the trailer and badly twisted the neck of the trailer and hitch. I showed her what she had done. Tears welled up in her eyes, as she wasn't sure what my reaction was going to be. Only minutes earlier I had warned her to be careful.

Immediately I put my arms around her and pulled her to my chest. "It's only a trailer. It's not a big deal." I could have gone the other way and screamed at her for being so stupid, for not paying attention to what I told her, or for not taking me seriously enough to watch.

Isn't it true that sometimes we get many things out of their proper place of priority? Pam was far more important to my life than an old ugly trailer. I gave her mercy. (Two years later, she showed me mercy when my addiction to porn surfaced.)

Instead of feeling we must punish or straighten out our mate, I believe we show the true spirit of Jesus when we forgive—that's when we truly show mercy.

If we decide to let the person off the hook, it's a risk we take. That person may never change. But then, if we go the condemning way, we have no assurance the person will change. In fact, we may further alienate that one. Or the person may temporarily change when we get angry, use threats, or criticize their behavior, but they will change for the wrong reason and it probably won't last.

Your anger should never be a driver of your spouse's behavior or that of your children's.

REPENT

If at this point you reflect on your life and recognize areas where you've used anger to drive or control your family, there is a simple solution. Stop! Ask your family to have mercy *on you*. I can almost guarantee they will. Two things will happen: one, they will be drawn to you and two, they will take your words more seriously.

You probably know that after constant criticism and confrontation, people begin to tune you out. Teens tell me this all the time. "He yells at me so much, I don't even hear him anymore."

Try letting your spouse off the hook and trust God to awaken her or him and give your loved one the desire to change. That change is God's job, not yours. Get out of his way and see what the Holy Spirit can do.

I'm thankful that God shows me mercy. I want to offer the same gift to those who offend *me*. Join me in this new thought, will you?

IF NOT YOU, THEN WHO?

If we established that we won't be the one to manage our spouse's sin, then who will and how? That is the power of accountability partners. One of the steps of accountability is the letter R from the acronym D.A.R.E. The letter R is to require action. It's where the rubber meets the road in accountability. As you set up your accountability partner, I urge you to ask this question: "What kind of consequences should we agree to when we fail?"

If you are serious about the relationship, you will come up with something that works for you.

Recently, I added to my arsenal of accountability partners a long-time friend. We had been meeting for only a short time, but we both decided to take this torment called lust and go after it earnestly and zealously. We bring our laptop computers to our accountability sessions every week and we hand them over to each other to review the Internet-tracking software. We both agreed to do this.

We look for any inappropriate sites that either has visited so we can lovingly interrogate each other if we find something questionable. We ask each other what the consequences should be. We both agree that we want total victory and purity. We both agree that we don't want to play games.

We considered fasting for one day for every infraction that we found. Another thought was to cancel any ministry engagements that we had within the week we found something inappropriate. We landed on this one: If either of us fell prey to porn, or anything inappropriate regarding lust in our lives, we would call the other's wife and let her know. Can you say ouch?

Even though Pam is there for me, I now need to know that every time I stumble there will be a discussion. For those of you who fear that giving mercy to your spouses will only enable them to keep on sinning, I say keep reading. If you take accountability seriously, and really want victory, then the objective is simple. You either want to stop the secret sin, or you don't. There is no *maybe*.

If you will not be the one to help manage your spouse's sin, then who will? The answer is: God, accountability partners, close friends, pastors, and counselors. If you want to try to change your spouse and are sure you can, I have two philosophical words for you: *Good luck!* You'll need it.

OTHER EXPERIENCES

Over the years I have had the pleasure of meeting with those people I call men of honor. I have met with pastors, lay people, new Christians, and seasoned Christians. Each experience has been powerful and life changing.

They took me by the hand and helped me climb the rungs in the ladder we call life. Each one filled a miraculous role at exactly the right time.

As my life changes and I continue to mature, I expect to meet with new accountability partners. The important success factor is trusting the process and allowing it to become a standard part of your life. Depend on the process more than on any one individual.

Chapter 10

WHAT ACCOUNTABILITY IS *NOT*

ACCOUNTABILITY ISN'T MENTORING

There is a distinct difference between mentoring someone and being in the position of equality with a person. I believe in mentoring; many of us have known those loving benefactors who saw possibilities in us and helped us.

I think of mentors as sponsors of champions. They see quality or potential in someone, reach out, and say, "I'd like to help." Those people can be invaluable.

Mentoring is also biblical. My favorite mentor is Barnabas. He's the one who grabbed Paul (then called Saul) and stood behind him before the leaders of the church. Because of Barnabas, Paul got his start. John Mark is another champion sponsored by Barnabas. He failed early in his spiritual journey by leaving Paul and Barnabas, but Barnabas embraced him when he returned.

Most scholars credit John Mark as the writer of the Gospel of Mark. He's a man of whom Paul later wrote to Timothy, "Bring Mark with you when you come, for he will be helpful to me in my ministry" (2 Tim. 4:11).

Mentoring depends on a teacher and a pupil. That means one knows more or has greater expertise in an area and is willing to share it. That's important but that's not accountability. Mentoring relationships are unidirectional and only last for a certain period of time.

I have previously met with others, and it sometimes took me awhile before I realized it was accountability: Either I mentored them or they mentored me. That's unhealthy when you don't realize what's happening.

If you're not sure whether it's a mentoring relationship, here are a few questions to ask yourself:

- **Is this person being vulnerable with me?**

- **Am I able to be vulnerable with this person?**

- **Does the other expose personal strife and sins?**

- **Does the other person avoid probing and pushing me to discover what is going on in my life?**

- **Is the other far more advanced in understanding and knowing the Bible, and I feel as if I'm the pupil?**

- **Am I going through a major crisis and meeting with that person guides me in what to do, but there's no mutual exchange? (Or perhaps the other person is going through the crisis.)**

- **Do our sessions focus on only one of us?**

If you answer yes to any of these questions, you're probably in a mentoring relationship. Don't knock it: If you need mentoring or the other person does, it can be helpful.

But a mentor relationship is not the same as an accountability partnership.

WHAT'S THE BIG DEAL ABOUT ACCOUNTABILITY?

I'm all for accountability and it is a big deal. Mentoring relationships can include accountability. When Cec mentors writers, he tells them exactly what he expects of them. But he says, "The traffic goes only one way. I direct everything to them and expect them to follow my instructions." He's not accountable to them, except to help them improve. They respond by reading his comments on their written work and working hard to meet the standards Cec sets for them.

Why do I make so much of this? Accountability works when both (or all) members are about at the same spiritual level. Focus on the word *mutuality*. It's like a partnership where both parties are co-owners. You need to be with someone who is at your level (within reason) so you can allow the core of your heart to be impacted.

For example, I know a situation with two men, lets call them Jim and Edgar. Jim had been a strong leader in the ministry for a long time. Edgar confessed a deep sinful secret because he was desperate, and his friend listened to every detail.

Jim was a great brother in the Lord and felt genuine compassion. He helped Edgar get his feet under him. They spent hours together over the next several months. Jim prayed for Edgar and was available whenever Edgar called.

That's a mentor relationship. Jim *mentored* Edgar through a crisis. Edgar got back on track and became a strong warrior for Jesus Christ.

One Thursday night about a year later, Edgar received a phone call. He learned that Jim had been involved in an adulterous affair for more than two years. This is a true story: Jim was having an affair the whole time he *mentored* Dave. The unidirectional relationship caused Jim to be vulnerable. It was a *one-way street*. It was obviously not accountability.

Did Jim offer good advice? He absolutely did.

Did his guidance help Edgar? Certainly, and it put him back in a restored position of ministry.

Jim was the loser. He gave himself to help Edgar, but he didn't open himself for Edgar to help him.

I met Jim after the heart-wrenching news so we could look back over the two years of his life. We both agreed that he lacked accountability.

Even though he mentored others, his life had been slowly strangled by the noose of sinful secrets.

Another angle to consider is to look at a few of the world-renown evangelists who have fallen to sexual sin. They destroyed their lives, their families, and their reputation. Worse (from my perspective) is that they brought disdain and reproach on the Christian faith.

ACCOUNTABILITY ISN'T HANGING OUT

Anybody can meet every week with someone and have lunch or coffee and catch up on the latest gossip or events of the other's life. They can talk about sports, God, or any other topic. They can enjoy each other's company, but it's purely hanging out.

Cec meets for lunch about once a month with a man named Win. It's purely an informal time, no agenda, no big discussions. They sincerely like each other. They usually talk about the books they've read and what's going on in their lives. Cec will quickly tell you, "It's friendship, but it's not accountability for either of us."

In such relationships, you may uncover areas where you can help each other, but that's not your purpose in getting together. It's not set up as a time of mutual accountability.

Guard yourself from falling into the trap or misunderstanding that just being friends and hanging together is accountability. It's not. I hear from many that this is a common conception. To guard each other's back involves intentionality and commitment beyond friendship.

That's one reason I offer the use of the D.A.R.E. method to keep you on track. (See chapter 8.) Guard yourself to keep it about accountability and focused on the person you are hoping to become.

Finally, you need to have someone hold up a mirror to your face and make you stare at it. It's not punishment or for the other to say, "Gotcha!" You also hold up the mirror to the other person. When you hear of the other's failure or weakness, you reach out. You do what you can for that person and expect it to be reciprocal.

For example, two guys I know met together for almost seven years. They decided that before they parted, both of them would commit to a course of action and write it in a notebook (both carried one). The next meeting between them started with the open notebooks. Each started with "This week I did…" or "This week I didn't…"

The best testimony I've heard about accountability comes from a man who said, "He lovingly opens my eyes to my blind spots and then helps me bring in the light."

Chapter 11

HOW DO I GET OUT?

I hear from many people that getting out of an unsatisfactory accountability relationship is the hardest part. To that I would agree.

Keep this truth in mind: Our God-given calling depends on our ability to surround ourselves with the right people who will help us succeed. Without those individuals, we can still succeed in life and still fulfill our divinely appointed ministry. But that's doing it the hard way. It's easier to have a partner who is at your side and who is also watching your back.

Why not use a method that can help you and move you forward in your spiritual growth? I'm sure many people look back on their lives and say, "I wish things had been different," and they groan about the bad times. What they often don't admit is that they themselves were the reason life wasn't different. Maybe they were ignorant about unhealthy relationships or naïve about the choices they made.

More likely, they were afraid. And it takes courage to open up to someone else.

If it is difficult to get into a healthy accountability relationship, how do you face the *big* issue of getting out of it? If the relationship is bad, you want out, or if it goes from good to bad, you want out. You also want out if you see no progress after several months.

In a mutual relationship of accountability, both of you grow. If there's no growth, something isn't working. And there are other times to leave an accountability relationship. Sometimes one person outgrows the other. That's common. Perhaps you feel the other person holds back from you. Or you may start holding back without being sure why.

In short, there are legitimate times to dissolve an accountability relationship. Let's talk about how to leave an accountability relationship.

DISENGAGE WITH LOVE

I want to stress ending with good feelings, with love, with appreciation. My first partner moved to Canada after five years. After seven years of accountability, Jim Martin moved to Cleveland. He and Cec had a celebration lunch together. "We disengaged with love," Cec said.

If you're unsure, here are some things to consider. Talk openly. "I'm not sure this is working for the best," is one way to start. Or perhaps, "I think we ought to examine our accountability relationship."

Ask questions like these:

* **How do you feel this accountability is going?**

* **What direction do we need to go in?**

* **Have you been getting as much out of this as you feel you need?**

* **How long do you want to continue this accountability partnership?**

* **If you think I've failed you, will you tell me?**

Be kind, but be firm. The other's time is as valuable as yours. Unless you have unresolved conflict, your friendship can remain intact and possibly become deeper because of the experience.

The best time to set up the environment for you to get *out* of your accountability is when you *start*. Tell your team or partner that you want permission from them to exit at any time with no hard feelings. Let them know your mission and how serious you are taking the process and they will be less startled if you feel the need to exit.

When Cec met with his group of six men, he asked them to agree on an exit strategy. "If you feel you want to leave the group, please tell us that you plan to leave. We promise not to try to talk you out of leaving. You come back the following week and give us a chance to have closure with you."

They agreed. One member, Greg, left after about two months because he decided to go back to college. (And another man replaced him.) Cec was the next to leave—after four years. He moved from Atlanta to Louisville, Kentucky. But he also said to the group, "I think it's time for me to leave anyway. I've grown and I owe so much to each of you. I think I need something different although I'm not sure what it is."

The others agreed with him and he left with good feelings all around.

Why not leave with love and kindness? In the D.A.R.E. acronym, the letter E stands for evaluate the progress. If you do this faithfully each week (or whenever you meet) there will be no surprise exits. I created the E step so you would have an easy way to exit the process. Use it as a tool.

I have departed from several groups over the years. Every person from those groups I still count as a friend, and we still respect each other. Getting out didn't damage my relationships.

By contrast, not getting out may damage a relationship. You may hang in too long; you may be afraid of hurting the other. By continually evaluating the progress, you can feel the dissatisfaction begin and realize it's a good time to leave.

Cec admits that after about two years he planned to leave the group and almost gave his one-week notice. "As I prayed about it, I realized that I didn't want out. They were pushing me to accept things about myself that I didn't want to admit. I had to decide if I wanted to push on and keep growing or drop out. I chose to stay and didn't regret it."

Satan wants you in shallow relationships, even with godly people. He seems comfortable if you want to have deep-rooted relationships with people who don't care about God or you. He constantly schemes against you, your marriage, and the calling that God has on your life. You have a Nineveh that God has called you to and there will be countless obstacles along the way.

Ask God to give you the courage to exit relationships that don't line up with your calling. But remember this warning: Be sure it's the right time to exit. Don't leave because you're uncomfortable. Make sure you leave for the right reasons.

Chapter 12

ACCOUNTABILITY IS A HEART ISSUE

More than 743 times the Bible refers to our hearts. If you read older translations, such as the KJV, you'll find statements such as "bowels of compassion" (1 John 3:17) because the Jews believed the bowels were the center of the emotions. Cec worked with a tribe in Africa that believed that center was in the kidneys. No matter what we call the center of emotions, the point is that we want to focus on the issues that get to the core of our being.

What we allow to affect our inner core is a big deal to God. Regardless of what happens to us in life, we want to avoid *hardening* our hearts. Hebrews 4:7 (quoting from Psa. 95:7–8) says, "Today when you hear his voice, don't harden your hearts."

Stiff-necked is another term used in many translations. For example, "The LORD said to Moses, 'and they are a stiff-necked people'" (Ex. 32:9 TNIV). The expression occurs several times in Exodus and Deuteronomy. In Acts, the first Christian martyr, Stephen, cried out to the Jews, "You stiff-necked people!" (Acts 7:51 TNIV).

Paul uses the same strong language. "Live no longer as the [nonbelievers] do, for they are hopelessly confused. Their minds are full of darkness; they wander far from the life God gives them because they have closed their minds and hardened their hearts against him" (Eph. 4:17–18). Quoting from the Old Testament, Paul writes, "For the hearts of these people are hardened, and their ears cannot hear, and their hearts cannot understand, and they cannot turn to me and let me heal them" (Acts 28:27).

Some versions of the Bible translate *are hardened* as *rebellious*— and that's what it means to harden our hearts or to be stiff-necked. The word means to become calloused or totally insensitive. In the biblical references the emphasis is on self-hardening: People choose to become callous and indifferent to God's will. It rarely happens in a single moment; it's more of a gradual hardening.

It's sad that people are separated from the life of God because they have hardened themselves. They ignored a few quiet warnings and pushed away the people who could help or challenge them. Eventually, they were so hardened, they could hear no voices calling them to repent or to change.

REASONS FOR A HARDENED HEART

I could list many reasons we harden our hearts. Perhaps the most significant is that we make a choice—a small, slightly off-center choice—to go our own way. That's the beginning of rebellion. Before we're believers, we have no allegiance or commitment to God. Once we become Christians, we promise to hear his Word. The Greek word for *hear* (*akouo*) has a stronger meaning than it does in English. To hear, in the biblical sense, implies obedience. So it's easy to grasp why we sometimes "say" we hear what we want to accept.

Sometimes God's will seems too difficult; sometimes it's just not what we want. Regardless of the reasons, there is within all of us the spirit of rebellion that we must constantly fight.

If we look at the story of the people of Israel, we see this clearly. They were miserable slaves in Egypt and God performed an abundance of miracles through Moses. The most powerful, of course, was the opening of the Red Sea for them to get across. Immediately God made the waters return to destroy the Egyptians who chased them. With that kind of history, wouldn't it be reasonable to expect them to obey every single command of God? Wouldn't it be natural for them to be so thankful that they'd be zealous to obey?

But they weren't. That's why Moses rebuked them for having stiff necks or hard hearts. The journey from Egypt to the Promised Land (with all the people, as well as their children and cattle) should have taken about a year. They were ready to cross the boundary of the

119

Jordan River when God refused to allow them to enter because of the way they had already disobeyed him at every point. In fact, because of their disobedience, they traversed the wilderness for thirty-nine additional years, unable to enter into the Promised Land.

How could that be? Why didn't they obey? Why didn't they fulfill their promises to obey God? Maybe that's not the right question to ask; possibly it's better not to ask about them but to point the fingers at ourselves. Perhaps the question to ask is this: *Why do we harden our hearts?*

Aside from what I've mentioned above, one thing seems apparent: I call it *protection*. We protect our hearts from getting hurt. We're afraid of pain and will do anything we can to avoid it. We don't want hardship or difficulty. If you make me mad or take advantage of me in any way, my heart can shut you out of my life. My heart can become like stone to you.

There is a natural mechanism in our brains that states the following message: "I'll erect emotional borders in every area. I'll never allow that person to hurt me again." We can erect the barriers, and we may cut out those whom we consider bad, but we close out the good as well.

That means the idea *doesn't work effectively*. We cannot allow our heart to become stony toward some without it affecting the others in our lives. Anger destroys the carrier, seldom only the target. Anger causes us to become blind and deaf.

Ask your accountability partner to help you evaluate those against whom you have hardened your heart. You may have a long list of reasons—and we can always find reasons for hardening ourselves—but we become the losers. We know how to protect ourselves against one person, but we can't stop with just one person. Once we open ourselves, every area of our lives becomes infected with stone-heartedness.

Don't focus on the reason a bad thing happened; instead, focus on the reason you want to change. Search your heart for areas of calloused buildup and ask God to forgive you. You may not feel like forgiving the one who wronged you. If that's the case, you might need to ask God to make you want to forgive.

Your accountability partner might need to help you to forgive yourself. Most of us have difficulty in forgiving ourselves. I often hear friends say, "By now I should have known better," or "I should have been able to overlook that incident." Maybe, but you didn't. Some self-centered, protective device within your soul makes you feel guilty. Regardless of how difficult it is, remind yourself that God wants to cleanse you and to soften your heart.

Ask God to help you to let go of the infraction. Maybe you need to ask your accountability partner to pray for you and to help you face your rebellious heart. Holding back may be the major factor that for years has prevented you from living victoriously.

One friend told me that he realized the one condition in the Bible in our being forgiven. We have to forgive others. Jesus said it this way: "If you forgive those who sin against you, your heavenly Father will forgive you; but if you refuse to forgive others, your Father will not forgive your sins" (Matt.6:14–15). The rebellious heart cannot expect to give mercy to another without first accepting mercy for itself. As you receive God's mercy and know you're forgiven for your failures, you're able to open yourself to others and forgive them.

It's like grace. If you've grasped the meaning of grace (which includes forgiveness) you can move beyond self-condemnation or self-anger. Until you realize how much God has forgiven you, you're likely to continue to harden yourselves.

Anger and a hardened heart twist us up on the inside and never lets us go. For instance, Betty did something that hurt you deeply. You were hurt so badly you just couldn't let it go. You held on to it, remembered it, rehearsed it in your mind, and told your friends about it. You thought about it often, but no matter how long you dwelt on the acts of the past, you could do nothing to change the present.

What happens when you're with friends and Betty's name comes up? What goes on inside you when you see her? That's what I mean by the twisting up. Your calloused heart keeps you from showing her mercy. By refusing to open up to her, you're hardening yourself from the joy of inner peace and from knowing your own sins are taken away.

For years I've promoted this concept with great results. Not only is it good to love those who "hate" us, it's important to respond quickly when our hearts are hurt. When a friend, spouse, family member, or neighbor does something that causes us pain, we can learn to react with love. Instead of trying to retaliate, offer them compassion. Forgiveness is mandatory for followers of Christ. Forgive quickly or you may become bitter. Forgiveness gives our heart back to those who hurt it.

For example, Pam and I had a big argument. In anger, I slammed the door, got into my car, and went for a drive. At first I thought of how she had hurt me (and didn't focus on how I had hurt her). That lasted about five minutes when I began to think about love. I did (and do) love my wife. My love didn't depend on her behavior or that she had to earn my love back before I could forgive her.

"I'm wrong," I finally said to God. I didn't hear a response, but I can only imagine a joyful voice from heaven whispered, "At last you admit it."

I decided to go back and apologize—more than that, I knew I *had* to apologize. I stopped and bought her some flowers.

But suppose I hadn't been able to admit I was wrong or to forgive? I might have gone back, pushed the pain aside (or inside) and Pam and I would have gone on with our lives. Yes, but my heart would have hardened against her—just a little. The memory of the words she said to me (and I probably would forget what I said to her) would remain locked inside me. I might remind her of that the next time we had a fight. Or I might just let the anger build. Each time she did something wrong—or that I perceived as wrong or inappropriate—my heart would build in a little more protection, which is called resentment. If I didn't change, one day my heart would have become so encrusted with resentment there would have been no place for love or kindness to enter.

GIVE IT TO THE PERPETRATOR

I've learned one thing that works: Love those who have hurt you. I want to explain that term. As you may know, there are four words in Greek for love. Two of them occur in the Bible, one of which is *agape*. It doesn't refer to emotions or feelings. It's an attitude. My co-writer defines it as *compassion in action*. *Agapao* (the verb) means doing what is best for the other person, regardless of feelings. It's serving them because they need your help. Jesus said it this way, "But to you who are willing to listen, I say love your enemies! Do good to those who hate you. Bless those who curse you. Pray for those who hurt you" (Luke 6:27–28). He says nothing about getting your feelings straight first. He says to do the right thing—and it doesn't matter whether you think they deserve it.

In fact, Jesus said to his disciples that the one way people would know they belong to him was by their behavior. Hours before his betrayal by Judas he said to his disciples, "So now I am giving you a new commandment: Love [*agapao*] each other. Just as I have loved you, you should love each other. Your love [the noun, *agape*] for one another will prove to the world that you are my disciples" (John 13:34–35).

For Christians, our command is to do the right thing for others because it is the right thing. In marriage, the perpetrators are obviously our spouses. Intentionally or not, they hurt us or fail us in some way. It's not just once but many times, perhaps regularly. That's just how it works. It could be a few sharp words. A task undone. A promise not fulfilled. A careless expression. Or it could be that we set impossibly high standards for the other person (and often don't tell them what we expect), so how can they not fail us?

Infidelity is the severe form, but that's not a beginning action. I'm convinced that a woman or a man doesn't decide one day, "I think I'll have an affair." It begins with small things, some of them I've already mentioned. One man told me, "I was unfaithful in a hundred ways before I committed adultery."

He admitted his big mistake (sexual sin), but he also confessed many, many little failures and acts of hardness that led to the big thing.

Here's what I want you to get out of this chapter: Get rid of the infidelity when it's small. Don't let it fester and grow. I can't believe a man or woman doesn't have some inkling when the other begins to turn away. If we love our mate, in the biblical sense, we do the right thing and reach out to her or him. If we do that, we stop the process that leads to sexual infidelity.

It can start with the irritation of her voice being too loud or too harsh. Maybe she makes her point and has to repeat it three times before she stops talking. It could be his lack of picking up his dirty clothes or his refusal to carry out the garbage.

Hardness of heart doesn't need much to get started. It's something of minor importance that irritates you and it begins to build. Once that seed takes root inside your heart, you start to count the times your mate does whatever it is that sets you off.

Before long, you see other ways in which your spouse irritates you. I'm sure you know how it works. Your heart starts to kick into the natural gear of self-protection. You don't want to be hurt again, you tell yourself. Instead of protecting yourself, think of this as the most crucial time for you to keep showing her *agape* love. Do the right, needed things for her.

My wife has said things to me in anger that hurt. Sometimes deeply. I've been guilty of the same rash behavior. Don't wrap a protection around your heart so that you won't get hurt again. Instead, do what Paul says: "And don't sin by letting anger control you. Don't let the sun go down while you are still angry, for anger gives a foothold to the devil" (Eph. 4:26–27). I want to repeat those last words. Anger gives a foothold to the devil. And it will if we don't correct it.

I've learned to deal with my anger and hurt with my wife within the same day. It's not always easy, but it is important.

Cec explains how he starts the move toward reconciliation. He points out that there isn't always an argument. Some people go into silent retreat. He says that when he's aware of being hurt, rather than allowing it to build up, he says to his wife or to a friend, "I was hurt when…" To start with "You hurt me when…" sounds accusatory and blames the other person for his pain. The focus then becomes what she did because she was too insensitive or too unaware to notice.

Cec says, "When I've started with the words, 'I was hurt when…' Shirley is usually shocked. She hadn't realized that she had hit me in a sensitive area. And we all have sensitive spots where we're vulnerable."

Even if you're convinced the other person hurt you on purpose, with God's help and with the prodding of your accountability partner, you can forgive. You don't have to let your heart harden against someone. As one of my friends says, "Don't give someone else control of the rest of your life by subjecting your heart to the vice of anger or bitterness."

The Bible teaches us to *love* our enemies. It doesn't tell us to hang out with them. It doesn't encourage us to put ourselves in harm's way. It simply tells us to *love* them.

If you're harboring destructive feelings, I challenge you to dig deep and find a way to forgive, release anger, and let go of the spirit of victimization that is controlling your life. Begin looking at tomorrow and close the door to yesterday.

Remember that not one person can navigate this vehicle called life by concentrating on the rearview mirror. For you to drive anywhere, you must look through the windshield and keep your eyes focused on what lies in front of you.

Giving your heart in love looks different in every situation. If you are a disciple, Jesus said his commandment is to love in such a way that we reflect the way he loves us. (That's the intent of John 13:35.)

Dr. Laura once said, "Stop whining and start living." I like that statement because it challenges us to keep our eyes on what's going on now and what lies ahead.

CONSEQUENCES

The consequences of allowing our hearts to harden are immeasurable. I have seen the most destructive events unravel in people's lives because of the onset of a hardened heart.

Many people walk into my office full of hurt, anger, and unforgiveness. They battle the feelings of victimization, guilt, depression, and anger. At times they are so consumed with how they have been offended that they can't see how it is affecting them or the ones they love.

A pastor was sharing with me about a woman who called to say her husband had tried to end his life by consuming a mixture of alcohol and pills. Meeting her at the hospital, they found her husband to be unconscious with little hope of surviving. His wife and children were shocked, not knowing what to do and what they could have done to prevent this horrific situation. After many grueling weeks of hospitalization and recovery, this man survived, but learned the hard way, the consequences of his hardened heart were not only life threatening to himself but caused a lot of pain and suffering for his family as well.

How about you? How are you allowing hurt, anger, or pain to eat at you from the inside out?

The consequences for your holding on to any hurt could spell infidelity, divorce, poverty, addictions, depression, health problems, pain, suffering, anxiety, medication, a miserable life, or loneliness. And that could eventually mean that death becomes more attractive than life. These consequences could be present because you held onto your pain and anger.

In summary, I challenge us to love in four areas every day. Ask your accountability partner to hold you to the following commitment:

GIVE YOUR HEART TO:

* **No. 1: the Lord Jesus Christ,**

* **No. 2: those who love you,**

- **No. 3: those who don't love you, and**

- **No. 4: those who don't deserve it. (That's what God did for us.)**

Be a survivor and not a victim. I have yet to see those who love and forgive freely and remain prisoners of their struggles. I have yet to see individuals who have shown mercy toward their offenders become prisoners to their pain. You too can be set free from a heavily burdened life if you find a way to show mercy to your worst offender and start letting your heart come alive again. Give your heart over to the Lord; let him deal with your struggles. Anger and vengeance are his to manage, not yours. Let it go and be set free.

FORGIVING YOUR OFFENDERS

Maybe those who hurt you most were your parents. The lack of love and affection from a mother or father (or both) has created a cancer in your heart that eats away at you day after day. The absence of their love and acceptance in your life left such a hurt that you have allowed your heart to harden. Scar tissue covers it up. You are in need of a heart surgeon and I want to recommend a great One—the Perfect One. His name is Jesus, and I promise you that if you go under his knife, your heart will be healed.

I want to give you a true example from my life to show you how grace and forgiveness works when a parent fails.

When I was a boy, my dad often took my brother Mike and me to visit his father, our grandpa. It wasn't a happy time for us because Grandpa seemed overtly angry for no apparent reason. For as long as I can remember, he lived alone. My grandmother's health was bad and she had been in a nursing home for years. I watched my dad tend to his father with a tender love that was simply amazing. He mowed Grandpa's lawn, helped him financially by paying some of his bills, and kept a close eye on his physical and mental health.

In all those childhood years, Grandpa never seemed to give my dad a single word of appreciation. And yet there seemed to be no limits to how my dad would care for his own father. Mike and I were too young to pick up on the little things that were out of place—little things such as we three were the only ones who ever went to visit Grandpa. I didn't understand why Dad would not leave Mike or me alone with him. When I was small I thought Dad might be afraid that I'd do something wrong.

My mom and sisters refused to go with us to visit, although they didn't explain the reason to me. I never saw aunts, uncles, or cousins at his place, which did seem a little strange. In conversations about the family, none of the family members ever mentioned him. When I'd say something about him at a family gathering, no one responded or had anything to add. It felt odd but I wasn't mature enough to catch on.

When I was sixteen, I asked my dad why no one else visited Grandpa. "Why won't anyone talk about him when we get together?"

"Sit down," Dad said to me and Mike, who is my identical twin brother. "I want to tell you about your grandfather."

When my dad was six or seven, Grandpa was caught sexually abusing his own daughter. Grandpa was convicted of child molestation and put in prison. From then on, all the kids were raised in various houses. Obviously, it wasn't easy for them.

After Grandpa's release and supposed cure, it wasn't long before he abused a neighborhood child. He went back to prison.

My father lived a lonely and tough childhood. As soon as he was old enough, he enlisted in the army so he could have a better life. And he changed and became a fine Christian man.

As I listened to the story of my grandfather, I was shocked. Then I became angry. I yelled as I glared into my dad's eyes. "How could you go to see him year after year and take care of a man who was mean to you and has done such horrific things?" My mind only imagined the abuse all the kids endured that no one knew about.

Dad took a deep breath and pulled out his Bible. He read the fifth commandment, "Honor your father and mother" (Ex. 20:12). He paused after reading the entire command and said, "God didn't make any exceptions."

He told me that loving the unlovable is a part of God's plan for his followers. I was amazed by my father's grace. He gave his dad a full pardon. He tended to his father even though Grandpa never returned the affection or showed the least appreciation. Not once did I hear my dad utter an unkind word about his dad.

Ten years after Dad told me his story, I received a call that Grandpa was dying and would live only a few hours. I rushed to the hospital and opened the door to his room. Sitting next to him was my dad, arm around Grandpa's limp neck. He was moistening Grandpa's lips with a wet sponge and trying to feed him a banana.

While I was still there, Grandpa died in the arms of his son.

At the funeral tears rolled down my dad's cheeks. After the funeral, I asked him what he was thinking.

"I will always wonder what it would feel like to be loved by a dad."

That's when I wept.

I would never have to wonder.

I tell that story because I saw love enacted before me every time we visited Grandpa, long before I understood the facts about him.

Dad hasn't had an accountability partner, but that says to me that the grace of God is so powerful, it can work without a partner. But all of us aren't as strong as my dad. I certainly wasn't. I can state without hesitation that I couldn't have done what Dad did.

And I'm glad I have an accountability partner. If I'm ever called upon to show that extent of love, I have someone beside me and behind me so I know I can do it.

If you find yourself struggling with unforgiveness, I would like to give you an assignment that could change your life. Write down the offenses that hurt you deeply. Be specific with each offense and put down details. Maybe you are holding on to guilt regarding things you did. Write it down. Whatever they are, write them, put the pages in an envelope, and seal it. Ask your spouse (or accountability partner) to go with you. Have a lighter or matches with you and make sure you have your Bible. Find a quiet spot and pull out the envelope, set it on fire, and watch it burn.

Ask those with you to pray for you and with you. Pray for forgiveness and the ability to forgive all those who offended you. Read Scriptures that are meaningful to you, then get up and walk away. This symbolizes your walking away from the hurt and pain as you offer forgiveness to each person or thing referred to in the envelope. For the rest of your life you will remember the day and place that you *chose* to walk away from a stronghold called the spirit of offense. You left all that at the feet of Jesus.

Remember, Jesus was brutally beaten, wounded, and nailed to a cross. While hanging there he forgave those who pounded the nails in his hands. He cried out, "Father, forgive them, for they do not know what they do" (Luke 23:46 NKJV).

Chapter 13

FEMALE BATTLEFIELDS

Cathy and Greg sat on the same couch, making sure there was space between them. Another subtle indication, perhaps minor to most people, was their crossed legs. It's not only that she crossed her legs, but her husband sat on her left and she crossed her left leg over her right—which pointed her away from him. His crossed the opposite so he faced away from her.

Can you picture that scene? I sat in a chair that faced both of them, Greg's body pointed away from her and from me; Cathy's body pointed away from both of us. Before either said a word, I knew we had trouble.

Cathy spoke first about their problems after six years of marriage. As I listened, I sensed her pain and confusion. (Men tend to have struggles that differ from women. I'll look at male problems in the next chapter.)

From the women I've faced in the midst of marital issues, I've learned they tend to focus on the quality of their marriage and the family unit. In the book *The Millionaire Mind*, Thomas J. Stanley states that slightly less than 50 percent of wives work outside the home. That's a considerably large work force. As he and others point out, even if women work outside the home, they still tend to do most of the work inside the house, such as cooking, washing dishes, making beds, and doing the laundry. Men often choose to do the outside work.

I mention this because the home is still where women place much (or most) of their time, energy, and emotion. Wives tend to focus more on children and family issues than their husbands do. I use *tend* because there are exceptions to gender roles.

I won't say my counseling is typical marital counseling, but in recent months, most of the couples that contact me for marriage counseling have a similar scenario. The husband is desperate for help, which, in most cases, is too late. He is willing to get counseling, no matter the cost. When I ask if his wife will attend the sessions, his answer is commonly no. He often admits that months earlier she had been willing to go for counseling, but he had refused. By the time the husband admits his need, many wives say, "Too late."

During the last year we have received an alarming number of phone calls from husbands. They usually start by telling me their wives have become indifferent or cold, have given up hope, and refuse any counseling.

For marriage counseling to work, it requires both partners to be willing to work at it. When one opts out of the relationship and leaves the other one to "get fixed," there seems little hope for restoration.

Where do those Christian women get that advice? Who tells them to bail out? My guess is that they listen to friends, family, or co-workers. "If he were my husband, I would…" is a common statement for them to hear. Some say it with even more conviction: "What you should do is…"

Instead, we need godly women who will fight for their marriages. We need to encourage them to honor their wedding vows. It may feel like a one-sided effort in the beginning. Too often they feel as if they are sacrificing alone to save their marriage and that all the work involved is on their end.

Older women can, and I think should, become advocates for the sanctity of marriage. They have the experience behind them and their marriages have survived, so they can encourage and teach younger women how to triumph during the challenging times and avoid many poor choices. They have experienced the turbulence, the peace, the hardships, and the joys and typically have walked with the Lord longer. Older women can function as strong mentors or as true accountability partners; they can take the hands of younger women and help them focus on the Lord and not the immediate circumstances.

Just because they're older doesn't mean they don't need accountability in their own lives. None of us can reach perfection on earth—no matter how long we walk with the Lord—and older women can profit from the give-and-receive relationship with younger women. Even long-time marriages can be improved.

WHAT IS YOUR BATTLEFIELD AS A WOMAN?

Most men and women have similar issues, but their circumstances are often different and they don't cope the same way because of differing perspectives. Many of the issues that we used to consider exclusively male issues, such as identifying themselves by their employment ("I'm a lawyer" or "I'm a pastor") now include women in the work force.

Most of the women I talk to work part time or consider the home their major occupation. The problems I hear often involve worry, especially about money, weight and diet, which are appearance-driven issues, business, critical attitudes, quick temper, keeping order in the home, finding quality time with spouses, depression, and controlling behavior.

I've asked women to identify their top two struggles. For them, it came down to self-image and emotion management.

SELF-IMAGE

If you're a woman, self-image and insecurity may be driving much negative behavior in your life, and you may be unaware of the effect it has on you and your family. That's another strong reason for having an accountability partner. The other woman can see what you either can't or don't want to admit.

Technology and society have influenced the perceptions of what a woman should look like and how they behave in the world today. You're pressured to be model-beautiful, which means thin yet healthy and maximizing your looks with little or no time or resources. You're also supposed to become business minded, independent, in control, equal to the male gender in self-confidence and ambition, provider, home manager, mother, and wife. It seems impossible for you to become all those things and feel as if you are following God's pattern for you as a woman, a wife, and a mother.

At what point do you:

- **value yourself as you are?**

- **learn to appreciate your unique abilities?**

- **let go of what others tell you that you ought to be?**

- **shout with joy because you have accepted that God made you the way you are?**

God has given you a significant purpose in this world, and there is no other person who can fulfill the role created for you. You may never be famous or wealthy, but what you do with your life matters—it matters to God. In his economy, your contribution is irreplaceable.

Here are Jesus' words: "Come to me, all of you who are weary and carry heavy burdens and I will give you rest. Take my yoke upon you… for my yoke is easy to bear, and the burden I give you is light" (Matt. 11:28). Jesus used that image because Jewish leaders commonly referred to the law as a yoke—and it was a heavy one. Jesus also offered a yoke, but he's saying that discipleship is a burden we can easily bear.

The Lord's words assure you that when you walk faithfully, the attitudes and opinions of others don't have to shape your attitudes or actions about yourself.

When you walk with Christ and disregard others' expectations, your self-image can improve dramatically. Depression can flee when you see yourself through the eyes of God and cast aside the self-imposed expectations that make you feel diminished.

Has frequent anger or criticism crept into your life? Consider digging deep into your heart and searching out areas where you use emotional anger or criticism to drive the behavior of your friends, spouse, or children. Do you find yourself frequently being negative or nagging until you get the behavior you want? And when you get what you think you want, does it satisfy? Are you a victim of serious hurts in your past that unconsciously drive destructive behavior and attitudes in you?

Satan would love to take you to that place in your life where you are hurt, victimized, or insecure and keep you there so you are disabled and can't be an effective warrior. Satan's lies—the negative tapes we hear in our heads—keep us from focusing on the truth of who God says we are. When you're angry or bitter, you harden your heart and push away the opportunities for the Holy Spirit to speak and to teach you. The Bible warns about developing a hardened heart.

Hardened hearts may well be the cause of millions of divorces in the world today. The hardness shows itself in the inability to really hear the truth of God's Word and apply it to yourself, to believe that God is who he claims to be and will do what he promises. "Give your heart a break," is something I advise. "If your heart aches, give the troubles to the Lord and let him heal you." Truth and grace are the only comforts for a hurting heart.

Could it be that you have a sharp tongue that quickly fires off rounds of ammunition? We all have the capacity to hurt others deeply with our words, with thoughtless and flippant comments that always seem to arise in response to our own pain. That's no excuse to accept destructive behavior that ruins or threatens family harmony. We can consider what we say before those words leave our mouths.

MALE LOGIC VS. FEMALE EMOTION

Men and women fight differently. I know there are exceptions to every stereotype, but it is helpful to identify the generalities that exist on both sides of the gender line. This is yet another reason to have an accountability partner of the same gender.

Men fight like a single-shot pistol. They can only think of one thing at a time. They see a problem, load their pistol with one bullet, aim, and fire. I like to think of it as male logic. It works in the male society. Sometimes they shoot each other and afterward have lunch together as if it never happened.

One problem with male logic is that women hate it. A man's technique is the opposite of a woman's. As a man uses logic to fight a battle, women use emotions. If males use the single-shot pistol, most women use a machine gun. They don't fire only one round but strike with rapid shots that unload the magazine. Critically wounded, many men are stupid and put another bullet in their little pistol and fire off another shot. In return, they receive another quick and painful spray of bullets. Both of them continue to fire until they feel mortally wounded. No one wins in a shoot out.

In retrospect, most men and women admit they didn't like the way they behaved in an argument with their mates. Even if one or the other declares victory, what do you really win? You may win an argument and lose the love of your life or the trust of a life partner.

Criticism and anger aren't productive. They drive your family's behavior deeper in the direction you don't want it to go. You *can* confront issues without the anger and criticism. You *can* learn different ways to address problems without emotion. There are techniques that have a long-term impact and will draw your family *to you* rather than push them *away*.

Every human being has blind spots—the negative things about themselves that stay hidden from view. That fact makes a strong argument for having an accountability partner.

If you have an accountability partner, ask her to help you control your tongue with gentle reminders when you are running off at the mouth. Be a wife who lovingly and generously supports and respects your mate. You want him to respond the same way, but don't base your love and kindness on his response. As one woman said to her friend, "I try to do the next right thing for him. Sometimes he gets it; sometimes he doesn't, but I keep on doing it."

Life isn't filled with easy answers to every problem, but the promised lighter burden from Jesus means you remain faithful and take the godly path. As another woman said, "All I can do is all I can do." And God honors that commitment.

EVERY MOVE YOU MAKE

The wise man says, "Charm is deceptive, and beauty does not last; but a woman who fears the LORD will be greatly praised" (Prov. 31:30). That verse implies that every decision and every move you make as a wife and mother draws your family closer to you or pushes them away. That doesn't mean life is always simple or the directions clear.

You may have bad days when everything seems to go wrong, when your actions seem useless, or you're blamed for what you didn't do.

But if you have someone to watch your back, that person can help you cope before you do something drastic and perhaps ruinous. The Lord holds you close to his heart. He knows your pain and discomfort and the answer to questions that seem to have no answers.

Too often emotional reactions to unmet expectations drive people toward destructive action and result in the opposite of what they wanted to accomplish.

Take this hypothetical situation. Brenda became increasingly upset because Bill came home late from work every night. They hadn't been intimate in weeks. The communication had become reduced to surface talk, and a sea of negative emotions built up inside Brenda. Bill seemed oblivious to her pain and whistled his way out the front door each morning as he headed off to work.

She needed Bill to spend more time with her, to connect on a deeper level, and to become one with her emotionally and intimately. She needed him to navigate his way back into her heart. If Brenda had shared her needs with Bill, he would probably have responded the way she wanted.

Instead, Brenda's anger built up—and she didn't have an accountability partner to cool down the anger. When he came home from work, she pulled out her machine gun and fired without giving him a chance to load his pistol. By the time she was out of ammunition, Bill's heart had hardened against the attack. He became defensive and finally pulled out his pistol. The situation worsened.

That kind of cycle of confrontation was the only strategy the couple knew. One or the other (usually Brenda) allowed anger and frustration to build up, and it struck like an overflowing volcano. Bill felt trapped and unable to do anything except scream back at her.

As one of my friends says, "Anger and criticism put us on a fast bus leading to nowhere."

I wish I could talk to Brenda. If I could, I'd urge her to find a safe, understanding woman in whom she could confide. If she chooses the right person, Brenda could learn to express herself in a gentle, respectful way. She might hold back when the lava is ready to overflow until she can talk and not overwhelm Bill.

A good partner can also help Brenda focus on Bill and his needs. His needs may be her blind spot. If she's constantly angry, whines, and criticizes him when he returns from work, how can they expect peace and warmth in the home? As long as she focuses only on herself and her unmet needs, she'll feel frustration or anger and he will be her constant target.

This isn't to justify Bill's behavior, because husbands play a huge role in the condition of their wives' hearts. The law of relationships states that Bill can only control Bill. He can change himself, but he can't change her. Brenda can only control her actions toward her husband. She won't ever change him. If that law is true (and I believe it is), both need help. Each needs someone alongside who can caution and encourage them and can speak objectively to their situation.

Your battlefield may be different, but the impact on your life is the same. Just as your husband needs someone to help him stare at himself in the mirror every day, you too need someone to push you to look at your blind spots—someone who can enable you to admit that you are contributing to both the problems and the successes in your relationships.

Your battlefield may be more emotional. Your life may be more centered on what you are *not getting* rather than what you're *giving*. It is easy to fall into a trap of being a victim to life and all you hoped it would be. Satan could be whispering in your ear every day, "You deserve more, you deserve better," and convince you to bail out of your marriage.

If Satan can derail you or your marriage, his chances increase in derailing your children and their marriages. That can result in generations of pain and hurt. Maybe your emotional pain hasn't been handled well and has driven you to inappropriate relationships or hurtful behavior. Perhaps you have sinful secrets. Nothing is over until you die.

Forgiveness is something needed by those who don't deserve it. Please read that again. That's how God works—forgiving those who are wrong, loving those who haven't earned it, and caring for those who have turned away. All of us need the grace of God to live as he designed us to live. As a woman, you need an accountability partner to help you reach that goal.

It's time to break the chains in your life and free yourself from the bondage of your secret fears and feelings. When you fight the urge to dive deep into the sea of despair and the emotional war zone, everyone wins. When you fight for the family to stick together, everyone wins. So for you and your battlefield, find a strong godly woman to meet with you every week. She can encourage you and challenge you as Christ guides her in wisdom.

Chapter 14

MALE BATTLEFIELDS

Now I want to address male readers. Here's my list of what I see as the primary issues men bring into counseling sessions. This is based purely on my observations and discussions with the men with whom I'm in frequent contact. It may not be scientifically verified, but it's what I hear when I counsel men.

The top categories men tend to struggle with are in the areas of lust, power, ego, anger, rage, passivity, laziness, commitment, and focus. Any of these issues can defeat a man. Where a man fights more than one of those battles, life can be fatiguing and discouraging. He needs help.

SATAN, THE BIG-BUCK HUNTER

I can approach this by looking directly at the human heart—and that's certainly viable. In this section I want to talk about Satan, the enemy of our lives. I use devil and Satan as interchangeable words, just as the Bible does. (*Satan* comes from the Greek, *satanas* and means adversary; *devil* is *diabolos* and refers to one who slanders or accuses.)

One thing I want to be clear about is that Satan doesn't tempt or battle at random. He attacks—and his arrows are painful and on target. But he shoots where we're vulnerable. I don't want you to blame Satan, because it means you opened the door and he sneaked in. While he is our enemy, he only has the power that we allow him when we don't lock the door. "Stay alert! Watch out for your great enemy, the devil. He prowls around like a roaring lion, looking for someone to devour. Stand firm against him, and be strong in your faith" (1 Pet. 5:8-9a).

Satan attacks the vulnerable. The susceptible. Those who are already looking in the wrong direction or those who don't have anyone to watch their back. I make a point of this because it's too easy to blame the devil for everything that goes wrong. A better way to look at it may be that Satan takes advantage of our weaknesses and failures.

Each man has certain weaknesses or proclivities toward sin. I've mentioned my own battle with lust. Many men don't struggle over that issue, but they're power-hungry or insecure, or angry.

Satan isn't capable of taking you out from a distance. He doesn't have a sniper's rifle or a weapon that can pick you off from far away. Instead he approaches us like a bow hunter looking for that big buck. A bow hunter can only shoot accurately up to thirty yards. That means that the rules of the hunt change dramatically. His power is in three areas: his location, his attractants, and his camouflage. We males—you and I—are the *big bucks*.

LOCATION

Before the Internet, if a man wanted to acquire something pornographic, he had to order it through the mail or physically drive to an adult store. If you're anything like me, you would not have done such a thing. Just the difficulty of getting to the material was enough to hold us back. Thousands of men who were warriors for Christ knew better than to get close to those deer stands. For most Christian men, walking into an adult bookstore or strip club would be out of the question.

But the Internet makes it easy. Tempting. "One time won't hurt," the seducing voice of the devil says. One time leads to a second and a third. Each time a man clicks on a porn Web site, Satan's arrows get closer and closer. The man himself walks into range and he's a big target. I can't go to the mall, drive by a billboard, or walk through the grocery store checkout aisle without seeing something that thirty years ago was considered soft pornography.

Or look at the ads that make us lust for bigger automobiles, more powerful trucks, or revved up Harleys. All lust isn't toward physical bodies. A man might steer away from an affair with another woman, but he'll all-but-sell his soul for a ten-cylinder Porsche or a Bugatti Veyron.

The location varies with each man, but the arrows are powerful and hurt just as deeply. Today, Satan has brought the most vile, corrupt, and graphic adult bookstores into the homes and offices of millions of godly people. Wherever that laptop or computer sits and allows access to the Internet is where his deer stand has been put up. Every time you walk by it, you're in his sights. His location has infiltrated into every part of a godly man's life. As soon as you click on the site, you're in Satan's sight and he's ready to shoot his arrows at you. If you have a strong accountability partner, the click on such sites can stop and you can overcome the temptation to peek at the site.

ATTRACTANTS

Scientists have studied the big buck with great intensity. Amazing findings have surfaced and exposed its power of smell and ability to remain out of harm's way. A buck has the ability to pick out one tiny human scent when it was masked with 10,000 other scents. It can sometimes smell a human more than a mile away. A deer uses the wind to protect its life because it usually walks upwind to detect danger through smell.

Bucks are nocturnal by nature, which means they rarely come out during broad daylight. The bigger the buck the wiser he is. He safely follows the herd or allows a younger buck to become his shield. The big buck is gifted with powerful senses and we wouldn't likely see the animal if it wasn't for that one time a year that he becomes totally stupid.

During the rut, or when does are in heat, the wisest of the wise become utterly stupid so that the sense God gave the animal becomes short-circuited and is overrun by testosterone. His ability to reason or to protect himself vanishes. He walks right out in broad daylight and the only scent his nose is tuned to is the doe just over the hill. That makes him totally vulnerable.

I write about big bucks because they behave instinctively the way many of us men act unconsciously. For example, I went hunting one year for the big buck and out walked an eight-pointer with a doe. Every move she made, he followed and paid no attention to anything else. He was so distracted that he lost all sense of danger.

They both lay down within thirty yards of my tree stand. I was hunting with a twelve-gauge shotgun. I watched them for more than an hour. She would get up to look around and immediately he would get up. She would lie back down and so would he. His focus was completely on her. She had his total attention.

I decided to fire off a round near them to warn them and get them to run away because I wanted a bigger buck. I took one shot and both jumped to their feet. In the excitement of my loud boom, she ran off over the hill behind him. He stood frozen looking in my direction. After a few seconds, he started to scan for her and couldn't find her. He started grunting as if to say, "Hey, where did you go?"

I yelled, "Get lost, you stupid buck! Run!"

He stared right at me.

I fired off another round and he continued to grunt and walked toward me. He was looking right at the end of a twelve-gauge shotgun and didn't care. As far as I could tell, the location of that runaway doe was the only thing on his mind.

I had my bead on him, I was a threat to him, and could have taken him out at any moment. I knew the danger, but he seemed absolutely oblivious. I thought, I can destroy all your aspirations to become the alpha male, granddaddy buck. Just then from the hilltop, the doe let out a cry. He spun around and they both ran to safety.

As I witnessed that display of the buck's stupidity, it hit me that the blind and stupid buck represented *me*. At one time Satan drew me into his range as I got on the Internet and started looking at porn. Every sense that the Holy Spirit put in me that was to protect and shield me was short-circuited by the testosterone in my body. All I could think about were those images. There I was, looking at the end of Satan's twelve-gauge shotgun and I didn't even know it. My spiritual life faced destruction while I sat at my keyboard blind and stupid and clicked on more tabs.

That's the point of the big buck story. If the buck had had a friend, another male, who could have yelled and warned him, he would have been safe from any hunter.

"Run! Get away from the hunter!" That's often all it takes from an accountability partner. I didn't shoot the buck, but I could have done it so easily. Satan isn't that merciful—he wants to destroy all of us.

As the hunter, I called the buck stupid and blind. "Don't you know the danger?" I wanted to yell, but he was captivated by what he wanted. He had no awareness that my finger pressed against the trigger could have ended his life—and his stupidity.

Are you and I much different? Probably not. Without someone to watch our backs, what we want (or lust for) can overcome our common sense. Like the buck, we get so caught up in our desires that we have no awareness of the danger.

But the devil knows and he's waiting to get us.

I escaped and so have others. So can you—and it doesn't matter if pornography, booze, or recreational drugs are the issue. The victory can be yours. But you probably can't do it alone—not if you feel strongly pulled away from godliness. If, however, you're committed to an accountability partner, you can stop the destructive process.

Paul wrote the wonderful promise of 1 Corinthians 10:13 that promises escape in the midst of temptation. What many fail to read is the verse that comes just before it: "If you think you are standing strong, be careful not to fall" (verse 12). To the Galatians he wrote, "Dear brothers and sisters, if another believer is overcome by some sin, you who are godly should gently and humbly help that person back onto the right path" (Gal. 6:1a). That's wonderful advice, but Paul adds a caution: "And be careful not to fall into that same temptation yourself" (1b).

In other places as well, the Bible warns us against temptations to fall into sin. If we become focused, like the buck, on some evil, we make an excellent target for Satan's arrows.

Satan will use a decoy, put on scent, burp his grunter, or use any other method he has to draw you out of the woods into broad daylight. He is a schemer. It doesn't matter which arrows he uses because they all have the same purpose: He has each of us in his sights and he won't give us a warning arrow. He's out to get us at every opportunity.

Maybe for you his attractants are friends at work, who may be outwardly nice people; however, if they cause you to think or behave in ungodly ways, they inadvertently become tools of the devil. Or maybe it's the uncensored sexuality on cable television; it could be email or magazines that cater to devaluing the human body and emotions. Maybe his decoy is the people in your life that you hang out with.

Internet gambling and gaming are becoming big, big issues. The people who wouldn't go to Las Vegas or to a riverboat on the Mississippi will go to sites on the Internet where they can gamble 24 hours a day. Others get hooked with games. A man I know spends at least eight hours a night on computer games. Those he plays are built on killing the enemy and stalking those who are out to get him.

The man has no home life. He begins to play when he gets home from work. He eats his evening meal at the computer and stays at it until long past midnight.

The last time I saw him he said his wife had left him and filed for divorce. "I'm not spending a lot of money," he said. "I like the games. They keep me alert and I've made a lot of friends on the 'Net."

"There are always ways to justify what you want to do," I said. I talked to him about addiction and that gaming had become the center of his life.

"I can turn off my PC any time I want," he said.

I wondered if he believed his own words. Or perhaps that's also part of Satan's hooks in him. But what if he had an accountability partner? Would that loving friend allow him to dismiss gaming so readily? I doubt it.

Regardless of where the enemy sets up his blind, you're always in his sights. You need help. An accountability partner can help you snap out of every temptation that distracts you and takes you away from God.

You may be like the big buck that is so caught up he sees or recognizes nothing else. Recognize the deep threat you're starting to walk into. Realize that on the other side of that decoy is the evil one and he has his sights on you. He is saying, "One step closer, one little step and I've got you."

By using this analogy, it brings us to the need for an accountability partner. By having someone near you who can pull you away, his arrows will miss. You may be distracted, but your partner can spot the stalker or the decoy and keep you from making a fatal step into the open field where Satan can control your life.

CAMOUFLAGE

Satan is a deceiver and very good at it. After all, that's his specialty. There may be people or situations in your life right now that are the work of Satan. Behind that person or situation is the mighty work of the deceiver and you can't see it. He hides behind the innocence of friendships.

Accountability partners can help you see the blind spots. So again I ask, who's got your back?

SO WHAT?

In order for victory to take place, you must expose your sinful secrets to someone. You need someone to see the blind spots and to stand back-to-back through the process of accountability partnership. Please find someone that you can meet with to share the sinful secrets that are looming in your closets.

EGO MANAGEMENT

I want to point out the area of ego. Most men struggle with ego issues from the moment they're born. They're constantly measured by material possessions, power, skill, athleticism, intelligence, body, physical looks, and the list keeps growing. The problem with success is that it brings with it what I call ego-growth hormones. Success in sports, academics, work, or dating convinces many men that they're the reason for their success. It's a sense of "I did it."

They don't shut God out of the picture—not entirely. They pause occasionally to say thanks, but deep, deep within, they believe it happens because of their skills, commitment, and effort.

God gets squeezed out of his life slowly—if he was ever present. Satan tries to convince the man that he is an awesome individual. He may send around others to tell the man how wonderful he is and how much others admire him. When a man hears words like that too often, he needs to be on guard. He needs to talk with his accountability partner and work out strategies so that he's not led astray by flattery or even by true words.

This matter of admiration is a serious issue. Cec has written books for many celebrities. One of the things he noticed is how many people gather around those high-profile people and constantly tell them how wonderful they are.

For example, one time Cec worked with a famous evangelist and wanted to observe the man in action. They were together and staying at a hotel. Thirty leaders for the crusade went into the hotel lobby and waited for the evangelist so they could have breakfast together. As soon as the evangelist and Cec got off the elevator, the people swarmed around the preacher as he walked toward the restaurant's private dining room. One man nudged Cec out of the way, so he backed up and observed those church leaders as they fought for seats near the evangelist. The worst moment was when one of the organizers grabbed a chair out of the hands of a woman and said, "I'm going to sit here." The woman had to find another spot—which was at the far end of the table.

Think about that situation. First, think of the attention given the evangelist. The more protected he became because of his celebrity status, the more open a target he became for ego inflation. All the attention, all the people flocking around, all the flattering words—

is it any wonder that he was affected by them? Is it any wonder that he became a prime target for a satanic arrow?

So far as Cec knows, the evangelist hasn't gone into any great, obvious sin, but he has become demanding and expects immediate attention and service. He expects people to do exactly what he wants.

And what about the thirty people? They were the decoys—the instruments the devil used to attack. But there was something else. They were as susceptible as the evangelist. In our culture, when people have contact with a celebrity, they seem to feel as if they have been elevated to a higher level in life. That is, Satan's arrows have also attacked them. They become like the smitten buck that follows the doe.

Flattery works. Deceitful, seductive words pull you in. And if you're not careful, your ego gets out of control and you don't know it. Many decisions you make as young men are based on ego. Possessions tend to hide the truth from your eyes and you can forget what's important.

Ego and male competition are ingrained in most men. I've often observed what happens when two or more gather. One man's alpha-male issues stick out and overpower the others with his achievements and win the spotlight. The form of the competition varies, but it's there. It can be who has the largest client list or who plays better softball. It can be who ate the most pizza at a tailgate party.

For example, one evening, four of us guys got together and sleep became a topic. In most male minds sleep is a feminine action; that is, "real men" sleep few hours. Women need seven or eight, but not alpha males.

During the conversation, one of them said he regularly got by on five hours of sleep. The one next to him said he needed only four.

The other two talked about their high energy level and one of them said, "Sometimes I get so focused on things I love doing that I forget to sleep."

I didn't get into the competition because I know I need far more than four or five hours of sleep. They probably lied or at least exaggerated. But I wondered how aware they were of what was going on. It was what we sometimes call one-upmanship. All the male ego instincts gathered and they competed.

If you're a man, think about the first five minutes after you meet another guy. What goes through your mind? If you don't know him, the usual first question is, "What kind of work do you do?" After that you want to know answers to these questions:

- **What kind of car does he drive; what year is it; what's the horsepower?**

- **How big is his home?**

- **How many toys does he have? Toys are things like sail boats, riding lawnmowers, motorcycles, or hot-air balloons.**

- **How much money does he make? He won't tell you the truth, but you try to size him up on that one. If nothing else, you'll figure it out because he'll drop hints about how much he spent on his toys.**

- **What kind of clothes does he wear?**

- **What does his girlfriend or wife look like?**

These may not be exactly the questions you ponder; however, many men struggle with the ego in one form or another. Once you get embroiled, you need to find some way or some level on which you're superior. And this isn't just a problem with those outside of Christ.

I want to point it out again: Unless you have someone guarding your back, you'll be right in the middle of the competition. An accountability partner can help you realize that you are fine just the way you are, even if you need nine hours of sleep a night. Does more sleep (or less) make you superior?

Jesus Christ accepts you exactly as you are; Jesus also works in you to change you. Sometimes the change either doesn't happen or it's like a slow-moving turtle. You may get so caught up in the one-upmanship that you seem to lose common sense or lose sight of what you want to accomplish.

As I said, most men start with a stranger and ask where he works. That method of communication is ingrained into males early in childhood. What they do for a living seems to be a big issue in the comfort zone of communication. You quickly compare yourself with others. If you have a better job or one that requires more education or pays better, you may feel quietly and smugly superior, even if you don't say that.

THOSE DEBTS

Much of your self-worth may be identified by what you do and how much you have. Success feeds your ego and sometimes you get into a rut that seems impossible to escape. The name of that deep rut is *debt*.

Debt is a terrible problem that men rarely tell others about. If you're typical, you can display your toys, but you don't show credit card statements or overdue bills.

If the male ego is the problem, what's the solution? One answer is accountability. A big step out of the debt pit is to share that ego part of your life with those who can relate and help. Ask them to help you to become a godly man. Your accountability partner can understand where you are and may be able to help. At least he's got your back and can protect you and gently lead you out of the danger zone.

WHAT IS SUCCESS?

Every year I now ask God to define what success looks like in my life. Here are a few of his answers for me, and in no particular order:

- **leading people to Christ**

- **serving the church**

- **creating unity where there has been division**

- **being a good husband**

- **spending money wisely**

- **reducing my personal debt**

- **loving people, especially loving enemies**

- **leaving behind a spiritual legacy**

- **forgiving people's offenses**

- **praying to God, studying his Word, and being spiritually honest.**

After I left a corporate job to pursue full-time ministry, my income was reduced by at least 75 percent. I was amazed at how I valued the dollar far more when I made far less. I didn't realize how cal-loused I had become to the collection of "stuff" (things I didn't really need) and spending for things I could easily do without. Somewhere between my motorcycle, bass boat, and loaded closets, I kept my ego comfortably fed.

I needed a good dose of accountability and my partner gave it to me. It takes humility to get an accountability partner. His loving confrontation was a test of my willingness to be corrected. My partner stayed with me and helped me grasp a proper perspective on my accumulated things. My leaving the corporate world didn't mean I had to get rid of all my possessions, but it did force me to do a double-check on my motives.

God judges us by our motives. Just as Abraham was willing to sacrifice his son Isaac, we need to be willing to sacrifice all we own because God wants to know the center of our hearts. That's another way to say that God wants us to acknowledge what we value most. Where is our ego and how willing are we to turn over our possessions and plans to God?

God wants your *willingness* more than your *possessions*. He wants you to be everything he has called you to become. To reach your spiritual potential you have to humble yourself and throw away, or move beyond, those things that hold you back—especially if they're things that give you a stronger status symbol.

Imagine meeting with a godly person of influence every week and that individual challenges you to discover the areas in which you can become more committed to serve God. Maybe it's at work where you need to let go. Maybe it's at home where you need to change. Regardless of where your ego runs wild, I'm confident that you can find a deep level of humility that can change your life.

Can you think of those who, no matter what setting they face, you can see that person's humility? A few people in my life are wealthy yet they walk with a great amount of humility. As I observe their demeanor, I frequently pray, Lord, help me be as humble as that person is, no matter how successful you make the ministry in which I'm involved.

It may be difficult, but if you are anything like me, you'll learn that the effort and the commitment are worth it.

To summarize, there is no room in a man's life for ego or lust to be present. Get an accountability partner to help you fight the ego and lust battles that wage war in your life.

Chapter 15

ACCOUNTABILITY IN MONEY MANAGEMENT

Many people tell me that they've had fantasies about winning the lottery or receiving a huge inheritance. Once they move in that direction, the question they have to ask is this: What would I do with the money?

And some people do win lotteries. Afterward, we hear horror stories of common people like us who win millions of dollars and within months their lives are destroyed by the newly acquired fortune. They lose control. They spend, spend, spend, and yes, they also give, give, give to friends and relatives, and tip generously—until the money is gone.

DEBT, THE NASTIEST FOUR-LETTER WORD IN ENGLISH

When we look at the total of all credit obligations combined (except mortgage loans), 37 percent carry more than $10,000 debt as reported to the credit bureaus.[3] At the end of 2008, Americans' credit card debt reached 972.73 billion dollars, up 1.12 percent from 2007. That number includes both general purpose credit cards and private label credit cards that aren't owned by a bank.[4]

"Americans who earn less than $10,000 gave 2.3 percent of their income to religious organizations," Smith, Emerson, and Snell write, "whereas those who earn $70,000 or more gave only 1.2 percent." While the actual giving percentages are slightly higher for Christians who regularly attend church, the pattern is similar. Households of committed Christians making less than $12,500 per year donate roughly 7 percent of their income, a figure no other income bracket beats until incomes rise above $90,000 (they give 8.8 percent). In fact, in absolute terms, the poorest Christians give away more dollars than all but the wealthiest Christians.[5]

Spending and giving. Those are two areas in which all of us can be held more accountable. Most people want to earn more, spend more, and occasionally give more. But they don't seem to factor in the need to be responsible for their money.

Shortly after Pam and I married, we met with Bill, a Christian financial advisor. He required us to create a list of our total income, total debt (indicating interest rates), bills, savings, and lifestyle expenditures. He spent a couple of hours teaching us godly principles of living with and managing money.

"No problem here, Bill," I said and smiled. "I don't have a debt problem." I was more than able to keep up with my two credit card bills, car loan, mortgage, and a personal loan from the bank.

"What is debt?" Bill asked.

I struggled a few seconds before I said, "Uh, well, debt is when you can't afford your monthly payments and you get behind. Debt is when you acquire too many loans."

Pam's face told me that my answer was less than adequate, but she didn't contradict me.

Neither did Bill. Instead, Bill taught me. "Debt is *all* borrowed money." He made that statement several times. He mentioned various kinds of debt: credit cards, mortgages, bank loans, friend loans, parent loans, and student loans.

While I absorbed that, he asked, "Can you tell me what the Bible teaches us about debt?"

"Uh, not to owe anyone anything," I said, but added that I was paying off all my obligations.

He smiled. "Yes, but until they're paid you are in debt to them."

The situation grew more intense and I was wise enough to listen.

After a few hours of discomfort, Pam and I decided on a five-year plan to get rid of *all* debt, except our mortgage. With God's favor, we were able to accomplish our goal in three years. Eventually we were able to save enough money to leave the corporate world and go into full-time ministry, thanks to Bill's ability to teach us godly principles of managing money.

BIBLICAL ACCOUNTABILITY

I share my experience because I think it's a significant area of accountability—and a topic in which most of us don't want to open up to others. So let's start with a few verses from the Bible about money:

- **True godliness with contentment is itself great wealth. After all, we brought nothing with us when we came into the world, and we can't take anything with us when we leave it (1 Tim. 6:7-8).**

- **Those who love money will never have enough. How meaningless to think that wealth brings true happiness! The more you have, the more people come to help you spend it. So what good is wealth— except perhaps to watch it slip through your fingers! (Eccl. 5:10).**

- **A person who gets ahead by oppressing the poor or by showering gifts on the rich will end in poverty (Prov. 22:16).**

- **On the first day of each week, you should each put aside a portion of the money you have earned. Don't wait until I get there and then try to collect it all at once (1 Cor. 16:2).**

- **Here's the command of giving a tithe (a tenth) in the Old Testament. The principle of giving to God started centuries before Moses gave the law and there's no verse that says God has erased that command: "One tenth of the produce of the land, whether grain from the fields or fruit from the trees, belongs to the LORD and must be set apart to him as holy" (Lev. 27:30). See also Num. 18:26; Deut. 24:22; Amos 4:4; Mal. 3:8-10.**

DEBTS AND MATERIAL THINGS

Some people may not be aware of their love for money even though they may be aware of their yearning for material things. For example, a few years ago I learned of a new housing development in the city I live in where $600,000 was the bottom price and some went up to a million dollars. New buildings were going up quickly. I wondered how people could afford such lavish homes. Our down economy didn't seem to support the new development.

A year later I spoke to a man who installed security systems and had worked in the new development. He told me about one family and said others were similar. The house was spectacular with every possible amenity: four-stall garage, huge atrium, six bedrooms, mahogany wood floor, marble counter tops, bathroom tiles from Italy, and all the other extras most people dream about having. There was only one little problem: They had almost no furniture. The house looked like a skeleton on the inside with one couch, three beds, one table, and not much more.

"Why is there no furniture?" I asked. "That seems odd."

The security man explained, "Most of them are living far beyond their means and they can't afford quality furniture. Yet they won't settle for poor quality or second-hand things in their luxurious home."

I thought about that for a long time afterward. Those families had their dream home, the status of living large, but no money left for furniture, vacations, emergencies, giving, saving, or college. That was a classic case where good accountability partners could have asked loving questions to guide them toward a more healthy life.

In a similar situation, a few years ago Cec lived a block away from what people called an affluent neighborhood such as the one I described above. He noticed that whenever any of them entertained, they rented furniture for the occasion. At Christmas, they had the most gorgeous and expensive displays in that part of the city—but on January 7, trucks came and picked up everything.

A neighbor said the people in most of those houses—childless couples—had nothing but bedroom furniture. Both worked and occasionally one of them lost a job. The couple had to sell the house because they couldn't live there on a single paycheck.

IS IT WORTH IT?

How do you rate your financial management system? What does it cost you to live in your dream home or have that sleek, fast, expensive car you've always wanted? Or the new Harley or SUV in your garage? Or does everything go to make you look good, prosperous, and happy?

Is it worth the debt and the worry? Have you paid too much and received too little in return? If so, perhaps you've invested in the wrong thing.

Is it possible that a portion of the money spent on your building or maintaining your lifestyle could benefit a worthy cause? Do you manage your financial life well enough so that you can give to your church and also give to other needs? Do you manage your finances well enough that you have zero debt?

I don't want to write these words to induce heavy guilt, but I want to push you enough for you to think carefully about how you handle your money. Is debt that nasty, four-letter word you hate to discuss? Do you dread the credit-card bills and the phone calls that remind you that your account is overdue? Do you handle your money or do your debts dictate your life?

IS IT WORTH THE WORRY AND THE HASSLE?

I urge you to consider your debt important enough to do a self-evaluation and let that be one more reason to get someone to watch your back. A spouse usually isn't the best person because he or she may be caught up into the same blinding storm, especially when it comes to money.

It also saddens me to realize how many Christians never give money to the church from which they demand so much. Some people wonder why God isn't dumping abundant blessings into their lives. God's blessings are conditional—they are based on our obedience and our giving of our time, our heart, our energy, *and our money.*

Cec told me that when he was a missionary in Kenya, one pastor wouldn't let several church members take the Lord's Supper.

"Why not?"

"Would you invite a robber or a thief to sit at the Lord's table?"

"Not if I knew—"

"Those people are thieves." In the Luo language he quoted from Malachi, where the prophet speaks for God and asks: "Should people cheat God? Yet you have cheated me!" (3:7b). In the voice of the people, Malachi responds, "But you ask, 'What do you mean? When did we ever cheat you?'"

In verse 8 God speaks again, "You have cheated me of the tithes and offerings due to me."

The pastor's actions were drastic, and I doubt that any western pastor would take such a bold stand. But I admire that pastor. His actions remind us that everything we have in life comes to us as gifts from God. Not to give back at least a tenth says that we're ungrateful.

If we want to live the abundant life Jesus promises, we can't ignore the money factor and the responsibility that deals with the way we handle our income.

Who is in your life to make you accountable for the way you spend?

Who's got your back?

Chapter 16

VICTORY IS YOURS

If you follow the steps of accountability throughout this book, you can break the chains of bondage. When you are able to accept the truth that you *cannot make it on your own*, that's when you can sense the chains falling to the ground one by one.

One thing that could make this easier is if you remind yourself that God wants you to have victory—always. You have victory available when you do things his way. "Those who trust their own insight are foolish, but anyone who walks in wisdom is safe" (Prov. 28:26). Wisdom here means to follow God's will.

For example, an executive called me as a consultant. The company wanted me to help resolve the conflict between a woman and her supervisor. We entered into the proceedings carefully. I allowed them to express their opinions. The supervisor said he tried to let the woman know he cared. He had reached out to her many times. "I wanted to help her professionally but also personally."

The woman came from a painful, abusive background. As soon as her supervisor finished, with tears streaming down her face, she cried out, "I don't need you! I never asked for your help! I don't need anyone!" She stared at him and yelled, "I've made it this far on my own and I am sure that I will be just fine."

Her supervisor stared back, dumbfounded. The venom of her words shocked him.

As it came out later in our talks, she was a frightened woman. She didn't know how to receive kindness or caring correction. The only way she knew to deal with such kindness was to distrust it and to lash out in anger before the other person could take advantage of her.

I wanted to shake her and scream, "It's okay to need someone!" But even if I had yelled at the top of my voice, she wouldn't have been ready to hear me. She carried so many painful memories that she didn't know how to trust kindness.

We were able to bring peace to the situation, but the woman never quite understood the positive caring of her supervisor. The sad thing I learned is that she had no backup—no one she trusted who would help her see her blind spots.

I'll probably never forget her screaming voice. The sad thing is that some Christians have such an attitude. They may not use those words, but in their thinking they have made it on their own. They seem oblivious to grace and kindness. "I don't need anyone. I'll take care of myself."

That's a lie from Satan.

You might want to argue that I don't realize how terrible or how painful a situation is that another person endures. That's true: I don't. No one else knows the depth of your pain. But God knows and cares. God reaches out to you constantly. And one way God reaches out to you is through your accountability partner. That person is not only there to watch your back but also to remind you of God's love and presence.

It's the lie of the devil that says, "You don't need help. What can anyone else do for you? You're doing all right by yourself." Even as he whispers those lies, he wants you to feel alone. Helpless. Unloved and uncared for. You protect yourself by listening to his lie that you don't need anyone. He wants you to expend your energies looking in the rearview mirror, *alone* and helpless.

By contrast, God has many, many ways to help you. I've written this book to emphasize accountability partners. That's not the only way, but I think it's one of the best and most simple ways. Accountability reminds you that you are not alone. You have at least one person who cares—one person who says, "I'm for you and with you. I'm guarding your back so you can go forward and not be afraid of an attack from the rear."

Accountability partners hold out the lifelines for you, no matter who you are. Roles in life—presidents, CEOs, pastors, parents, or singles—are only the situation in which you live. The accountability partner promises to walk beside you and behind you no matter what battles you face.

THE POWER OF CONFESSIONS

"People who conceal their sins will not prosper, but if they confess and turn from them, they will receive mercy." Proverbs 28:13 promises mercy, and that includes forgiveness and peace.

Again, I'll write about myself. I'm zealous for accountability partnership because I know it works. I'm constantly aware of what it's done for me and how it has strengthened me. When I began to expose my sinful secrets to my accountability partner, I experienced the power of freedom and inner joy. I no longer cared if anyone found out about some of my inmost secrets. In fact, I no longer harbored those secrets. I had failed; I had done many wrong things.

But once I stopped denying my failures and began to expose them to the light, they no longer held any power over me. I needed—honestly needed—another person to hear my confession and, as a representative of Jesus Christ, that man told me I was forgiven.

He read verses such as this: "If we claim we have no sin, we are only fooling ourselves and not living in the truth. But if we confess our sins to him, he is faithful and just to forgive us our sins and to cleanse us from all wickedness. If we claim we have not sinned, we are calling God a liar and showing that his word has no place in our hearts" (1 John 1:8–10).

It is in confessing my failures to another and hearing the assurances of pardon and acceptance that I am freed from my secrets and from my past.

I no longer have secrets because I can use my failures to glorify God by telling others about my bondage and the freedom I found in Jesus Christ.

I can tell them two powerful truths:

1. I am forgiven.

2. I am free.

I'm not the righteous man who has never fallen, and neither are any of us. I'm not the Pharisee of Jesus' day, who obeyed every law and made keeping the law his purpose in life.

I'm a sinner who deserves punishment and eternal damnation, but God didn't give up on me. I still fail at times, but I also know that when I'm weak, I can call on the one who strengthens me and lifts me up. Again to quote Paul, "I can do everything through Christ, who gives me strength" (Phil. 4:13).

At times I'm like a wounded soldier who keeps getting up, but sometimes I'm so wounded, I can only stand with the help of other soldiers. *I'm not alone.* I have the Holy Spirit to lead me forward and my accountability partner to guard my back. I'm a warrior who desperately needs other warriors by my side. I'm a warrior who understands that my family needs me to humble myself to other warriors and subject myself to their rebuke.

I've been set free from the bondage of pornography and various other sins because I repented and asked a fellow warrior to help me. Other sinful secrets will enter into my life—the devil constantly seeks entry—but I know I'll have that friend with me who will help me expose my sin and repent.

When we expose our sinful secrets to someone and ask God to forgive us, we receive the gift of freedom. No other formula works. No medicine, no self-anger, no amount of running away or crying, no books, no revenge, and no hiding will save us. Repentance before God and continued exposure to a fellow Christian warrior become the two parts of the true formula that works for me and for others.

AN EXAMPLE OF VICTORY

Years ago my friend Tim called me because his marriage was failing, and he asked for help. We talked for a long time, but the essence of it was that he no longer loved his wife and wanted a divorce. Months earlier, Tim had promised to be accountable. (I wondered why it took him so long to do what he had promised.) He hadn't gotten involved with another woman. They had two children, whom he still loved. He and his wife had been involved in a high level of conflict and one that had been going on for months.

"I just want out. I want peace and the opportunity to find a woman whom I can love and live with for the rest of my life."

"Have you verbalized your feelings to your wife?"

"Yes," he said quietly.

I'd known Tim for several years and respected him highly. He had a promising career as a doctor and was a man of outstanding character.

"I'm weary. I just want out."

"The decision is yours," I told him in what I felt was a firm, loving way, "but you are doing a terrible thing to remove the single most important element a wife needs." I tried not to tell him what to do—he had to make that decision—but I did point out that his wife needed emotional security. "She needs security that comes through your commitment and loyalty."

I urged him to go home and not to use the "D" word again. When we throw the word *divorce* around it causes the same damage a wrecking ball does to a building. At its minimum it's a threat that hangs over a relationship.

I asked him to quit thinking about *his* needs and *his* feelings and start serving *her*. He committed himself to do the things I suggested for the next three months.

When we fall out of love, it is a sign that we've stopped serving our spouse. We need to understand that our feelings are a direct result of our actions. When we first choose to act *in love* to our spouse, our feelings follow in time. When we choose to act on *our feelings* instead of our behavior, we are in deep trouble. As I pointed out earlier, true love—*agape*-love—is an attitude—it's action intended for the good of the other.

We need to be careful about our feelings. My co-writer says it this way, "My feelings are emotions; my feelings are not reality." For example, I may feel worthless, but that doesn't make me useless. It means I'm listening to my feelings rather than looking at reality and listening to God. Too often feelings are a reactive force to the variations of life and our actions.

Tim took my advice. For three months he tried to become the best husband he could be. He asked his wife to forgive him for hurting her with the threat of divorce and promised that he would not use the word again.

About a year later Tim called. He and his family had moved away, but he called to thank me for loving him enough to speak to him so candidly. He delivered great news that his love affair with his wife had never been stronger. He fought his way back to being in love with her. Later he said that their love was even stronger than before. His *chains were broken* due to the courage he had to expose his secrets to another man who loved him enough to speak the truth, and his own ability to repent.

Where would Tim have been without an accountability partner? Where would Tim and his family be if he had talked to no one but went on his projected path?

Where will your life end up if you remain disconnected from accountability?

THE POP-UP GAME

Have you ever gone to Chucky Cheese with your children? More than just the pizza is a game there called Pop-up. It has a soft sledgehammer chained to the machine and characters pop up. As soon as they do, you hit them as hard as you can so they go down. The longer the game goes on, the faster they pop up.

It's great exercise and a lot of fun to keep going. And as I play that game with my young nephews and nieces, I'm reminded that Satan works like that in our lives. We think everything is all right and then up he pops. It seems as if the moment we smash one sin down and claim victory he tempts us in a different area.

We spend our life smashing sins like the pop-up game. We get weary and at times we want a break, or sometimes we say, "I'm too tired to keep going. I want to quit."

What is true victory? How do we get out of the pop-up game? We won't entirely get out as long as we live, but I believe that accountability will help us. I can say this from my own experience and relate it from the experience of others: Accountability has helped me slow down the pop-up temptations and sins. I may not stop them, but they seem to pop up less often or catch me by surprise less frequently. I have someone at my side and he can use his hammer when I'm too weary to use mine. Between the two of us, I can always win.

If you are a leader of any kind, I want to share with you the freedom that can exist in your life. Over the past fifteen years I've been involved in leadership in the corporate world and the ministry. Without accountability in my life, I felt as if there were a thick cloud between the people I was leading and me. I couldn't understand it.

One time a woman sent me a note that read, "I love your passion and your words, but it would mean more to me if you would love us up close and not from so far away." Those words hurt, but she was right. That loving rebuke took me years to figure out and learn to open myself more fully. At the time, unresolved sin was a big factor. I was also afraid to trust others and to open myself. What if they didn't like me? What if they rejected me?

But we can get beyond those unresolved issues. We can break down the barriers that separate us from others. We not only need to repent, but we also need to leave the old ways. Often, the accountability person is the one who holds our hands as we leave the old way.

Accountability has helped me to find victory where nothing else worked. The absence of habitual sin will yield the feeling of victory.

Some critical person once said, "Every preacher who struggles with sin should step down from preaching." If that were to happen, every preacher in the world would have to stop. The issue isn't struggling with sin; the issue is that they fail when they allow sin to overtake them. That's the time to step aside. But all of us—

preacher or lay person—struggle with pop-up sin. We can't stop the popping up, but we can become strong and responsible enough to hammer the sins that pop up.

Victory rests on the other side of confessing. If we allow fellow Christians to walk with us and know our sin so that we may repent to our Lord in heaven, we will feel the wind of forgiveness and sense the sweet taste of victory. When we speak to others, we want to be used by God. Then his fullness can flow through us with no chains wrapped around our bodies. With divine power energizing us, we can fight the good fight.

SATAN WANTS ALL LEADERS TO BE BOUND

Imagine how terrible, perhaps embarrassing, it would be if someone opened your closet door and exposed all your dirt. Trust me, I've been there. Maybe you are in some kind of bondage and it feels like there is a chain wrapped around your neck or ankle that is holding you back.

Remember that Satan is more fervent with the spiritually zealous than he is with others. Please fight back. Find the courage to expose your hidden sins and watch Satan run from you. Keep telling yourself that it's the secret, not the sin. The chains are the secrets, the bondage is the secret, and victory is the exposure.

Life is really simple, but here's an easy question. Would you rather remain in bondage or have a partner to help you win over your jailer? Perhaps that's even too simple to ask, but that's still a viable question. When we can't win battles by ourselves we can enlist the help of others—our accountability partners.

I hate what the devil does to pastors and leaders in the ministry. I'm on the front lines of battle standing back to back with you. I hope this book is nothing short of a sword that God has put in my hand. As you read it imagine me standing back to back with you piercing the demonic forces that keep you in the prison of bondage.

MY PRAYER FOR YOU

Lord, give all readers your mercy and forgiveness. Thank you for your power through the Holy Spirit that can help them expose sinful secrets to other godly friends who will petition you on their behalf.

Make accountability a significant part of their lifestyle so they may continue to experience a deeper relationship with you. I pray that bondages will be broken, hearts be softened, and forgiveness be given to their offenders. Amen.

FINAL THOUGHTS

I hope you found this book to be life changing.

Please contact me to share how you benefited by reading this book. My Web address is www.daretobedifferent.com.

END NOTES

1. Public Broadcasting Service (PBS), "Depression, Out of the Shadows: Statistics," http://www.pbs.org/wgbh/takeonestep/depression/pdf/dep stats.pdf (accessed January 15, 2009).

2. Effects of Pornography Addiction on Families and Communities, James B. Weaver, III, http://www.obscenitycrimes.org/Senate-Reisman-Layden-Etc.pdf

3. www.myfico.com

4. Nielson Report, April 2009

5. http://www.christianitytoday.com/ct/2008/december/10.24.html?start=2

ABOUT THE AUTHORS

MATT LOEHR has a degree in electronic engineering and for 18 years worked for a worldwide corporation as a computer/electronic engineer. Matt found his way into a leadership role and spent the majority of his years leading, training, and equipping others in his field.

MARRIAGE MINISTRY: Matt and his wife, Pam, left their careers and founded Dare to Be Different, Inc., a nonprofit organization that focuses on strengthening families by empowering marriages.

Matt and Pam became certified marriage mentors after receiving training from PREP, FOCCUS, and Biblical Portrait of a Marriage. They created the D.A.R.E. Marriage Mentoring System that is designed to mentor premarital and at-risk couples. Their goal is to train 100,000 mentors using this system.

SPEAKING ENGAGEMENTS: Ordained in 2009, Matt is a dynamic preacher. He is on a team of speakers for a men's ministry called Crosstrainers and speaks for Iron Sharpens Iron, a national men's ministry.

MOODY RADIO/TELEVISION: Matt provides a weekly program on Moody radio that helps couples find ways to deal with issues that many marriages and families face in today's culture. Matt and Pam have also provided marriage tune-ups on a local television program.

HOBBIES: Matt loves to bow hunt whitetail deer in Iowa as well as bass fish wherever and whenever he gets the chance. Pam enjoys the outdoors, gardening, hiking, kayaking, and bike riding.

If you are interested in developing marriage mentors in your church or would like to schedule Dare to Be Different for your marriage banquets, weekend retreats, or conferences, contact Dare to Be Different at 1-877-813-7518. If you are interested in becoming a regional trainer or learning more about Dare to Be Different, visit www.daretobedifferent.com.

Who's Got Your Back?, a nine-week study guide, is available. Designed to stimulate accountability relationships in churches, the study guide is interactive and holds the participants accountable to action. When Christians become accountable to each other, the burdens are greatly lessened for the pastors and leaders.

The study guide is available online at www.daretobedifferent.com.

CECIL (CEC) MURPHEY is the author or co-author of more than 100 books, including the New York Times bestseller *90 Minutes in Heaven* (with Don Piper) and *Gifted Hands: The Ben Carson Story* (with Dr. Ben Carson). He is also the author of the following recent releases: *When God Turned Off the Lights*, *60 Seconds to Greatness* (with Eddie Long), *Christmas Miracles*, *When Someone You Love Has Cancer*, and *Words of Comfort for Times of Loss*.

His books have sold millions of copies and have brought hope and encouragement to people around the world.

Cecil stays busy as a professional writer and mentor and travels extensively to speak on topics such as Christian living, recovery, spiritual growth, prayer, caregiving, significant living, male sexual abuse, and writing.

Prior to becoming a full-time writer and speaker, Cecil served as pastor of Riverdale Presbyterian Church in Metro Atlanta, as a volunteer hospital chaplain for ten years, and was a missionary in Kenya for six.

For more information about Cecil Murphey, visit his Web site at www.cecilmurphey.com.

StRenGtHeninG MaRRiaGeS:

Other Products and Services from Matt and Pam Loehr

MaRRiaGe MentORinG: Find the necessary tools to mentor premarital and at-risk couples using the D.A.R.E. mentoring system (Discover, Ask, Require, Evaluate).

DiSCOVeRY CaRDS: Have you come to the place in your relationship where you feel like you no longer have anything to talk about? If so, Discovery Cards can help renew your relationship through thought-provoking, as well as humorous and light-hearted questions. This creative communication tool will strengthen your relationship in a fun and non-threatening way.

COnFeRenCeS/BAnQUetS: Call 1-877-813-7518 to book an event or go to www.daretobedifferent.com to learn more about all products and services.